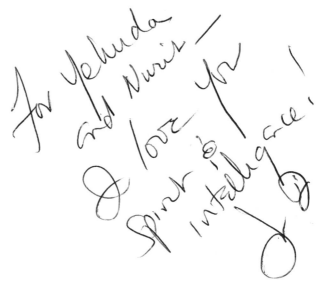

The Spoon from Minkowitz

A Bittersweet Roots Journey to Ancestral Lands

Judith Fein

The Spoon from Minkowitz: *A Bittersweet Roots Journey to Ancestral Lands*

By JUDITH FEIN

Copyright ©2014 Judith Fein

A GlobalAdventure.us book

P.O.B. 31221
Santa Fe, NM 87594
http://www.GlobalAdventure.us

Printed in the United States of America

Interior Photography by Paul Ross
Cover design by Susan Paradise
Cover photo by Paul Ross

ISBN: 978-0-9884019-3-8

Contents

INTRODUCTION

Dear Reader,

Ever since I was a child, I was obsessed with Minkowitz, the village my grandmother came from in Russia. She didn't want to talk about it. The less she revealed, the more I wanted to know. Like a young dentist, I extracted six facts from her, and I clung to them all of my life. When I grew up, I developed into a schleppy sleuth in a detective story, pursuing the six clues and slowly, slowly getting closer, but I was never able to solve the mystery of Minkowitz.

The village wove in and out of my life in bizarre ways. I wondered if it were real, if it still existed, if the fiddler, so to speak, was still on the roof. I became a playwright and wrote a play about it. I realized that what I actually knew was very flimsy. Six facts. I repeated them over and over, like a theatrical mantra.

Then I became a travel writer. I journeyed all over the globe, but never went to the village. I was afraid of what I would find and what I wouldn't find. Maybe it was better to leave it alone as a construct of my febrile imagination.

And then, a year ago, I was on a trip that was a few hours from Ukraine, where the village is located today. I found a guide. He provided a car. Armed with the same six clues, I went. And what happened to me changed my life.

I would be disingenuous if I didn't tell you that I had an ulterior motive in writing this book. I want you to come along with me, to experience what I saw, felt, heard, stumbled upon, and understood. I want to introduce you to the people I met. I want to open up to you a world that made me laugh and learn, wonder and weep.

And then, one day, I would like you to undertake such a voyage yourself….to the land your ancestors came from. It will help you to better understand who you are, and honor what and who came before you.

Even if your ancestors are long gone, they are still within reach. Waiting. Waiting. Calling out. And all you have to do is heed the call, pack your bags, and go back into the past to find what is there, waiting for you.

Judith Fein

The Spoon from Minkowitz

The author, flanked by her mother and grandmother, in the latter's Brooklyn home.

CHAPTER ONE – SIX FACTS

W hen I was 10 years old, while other girls were playing with dolls, I was obsessed with the *shtetl,* or village, my grandmother came from. I begged my parents to take me to Brooklyn, so I could sit next to her, feel the softness of her skin, and ask her about her village in Russia.

My grandmother was not forthcoming. Nor did she know exactly where her *shtetl* was located because it was an isolated village, and the only time she ventured any real distance from it was to come to the United States when she was 17.

"Grandma, where do you come from?" I would ask.

"Far."

"What was it like?"

"Feh."

The less she said, the more my imagination went wild, conjuring up images of a dark, mysterious place in Russia with sinewy alleys. I was awed that my grandmother, the woman who was my mother's mother and called me *"mamaleh,"* lived in such a place and knew its secrets.

"Please, Gram, tell me."

"It's better to forget about it."

She never spontaneously talked about Minkowitz, and I never gave up questioning her or trying to find out about her life before she came to America, before I knew her. Who was she before she was my grandmother?

"Tell me what you ate there, Gram."

"Food."

"Where did you buy it?"

"There was a market once a week, on Tuesdays. We had beans, potatoes, beets, corn...." her voice trailed off. She went into the kitchen to stir the chicken soup, and I watched the yellow chicken legs float to the surface and then disappear.

"Are you hungry, *mamaleh*?" she asked.

When I nodded, she opened the refrigerator and took out a jar full of *schmaltz*—rendered chicken fat—that was speckled with burnt onions. She spread half an inch of *schmaltz* on a piece of rye bread, and handed it to me.

"Did you eat *schmaltz* in Minkowitz?"

She nodded yes. I took a huge bite of bread, relishing the *schmaltz*, because it linked me to my grandmother's village.

I was never very interested in religion, but I loved everything about my grandmother's culture: the Yiddish newspaper that was folded up on an overstuffed, upholstered armchair in the living room; the front parlor, where I slept, and which looked out over the street; the pantry closet which smelled vaguely from matza. Most of all, I loved that she came from Minkowitz. It sounded so exotic. It was somewhere across the ocean, in a vast country called Russia. She

2

wasn't born in America, like I was. She came from a mysterious place and she was a foreigner with secrets. I felt about her the way the ancients must have felt about travelers who arrived in their midst; they wanted to hear stories, to learn about how people lived in faraway lands. The slightest details that my grandmother divulged about Minkowitz became indelibly imprinted on my brain.

"Gram, did you go to school?"

"No, *mamasheyna.*"

"Why not, Gram?"

"We weren't allowed to."

"Why couldn't you go to school?"

I was like a little prosecuting attorney, and my grandmother softened on the witness stand. She got a faraway look in her eyes.

"I stood at the bottom of the hill, looking up at the school where the Russian girls studied. They wore blue uniforms. I wanted to be educated like them."

"But you couldn't….?"

She shook her head no. I wrote down everything she told me, and thought about it until the next time I saw her. Then I started asking questions again.

"If you didn't go to school, what did you do all day in Minkowitz?"

"When I was 10 years old, like you are now, I was working."

"What kind of work?"

"I dried tobacco leaves in the field with the women."

I had never seen a tobacco leaf. Why did they need to be

dried? I wrote down what my grandmother told me, and mulled it over until our next conversation. My mother said I was making my grandmother crazy. I didn't understand what I was doing wrong. I loved my grandmother. I was just asking her about her childhood.

"Tell me about your house, Gram. What did it look like?"

"The floor was made from goat dreck."

Goat shit for a floor. Were there clumps of dung? Who spread them out? Did they stink? What happened if you walked on the floor with bare feet? I clung to each tidbit, marinating it in my mind and imagination, repeating it to myself as though my life depended upon my remembering it.

On one visit, I was playing with cans of food in my grandmother's hall closet, stacking them, and unstacking them, using them like big tin Legos. She walked by and patted me affectionately on the shoulder.

"Where in Russia was Minkowitz, Gram? Do you know the name of the biggest city in the area?"

"*Oy*. Always Minkowitz. The biggest city was Kamenetz Podolsk."

Again, I wrote down every word she said. I thought I was getting ancestral gems, but later, when I looked at the content, it was paltry indeed. No stories. No slice of life anecdotes. Just six facts about my grandmother's life in Minkowitz. That was it. The weekly market was on Tuesday. When she was 10 years old, she dried tobacco leaves with the women. She lived at the bottom of a hill. The Russian girls went to school on top of the hill. The floor of the house was made of goat dung. Kamenetz Podolsk was the big town. I repeated the scant facts over and over, clinging to them, imagining what they looked like, felt like, smelled like. It was so vivid that I felt as though I had lived in Minkowitz too.

I knew that in Minkowitz they spoke Yiddish. I started trying to imitate the sounds of the language since I couldn't speak it. Instead, I invented a sort of fake Yiddish. I would call my grandmother, and, when she answered the phone, I would cheerfully ask, "Grandma, *vus habastups-du?*"

"Judie," she would say sadly, "I don't understand your *Eedish.*" That's how she pronounced it: "*Eedish.*"

The next time I called, I greeted her with the bogus, "Grandma, *hoison boisin galempt.*"

"Judie, I'm sorry. I just can't understand your *Eedish.*"

When I was 19, bedridden with mononucleosis and hepatitis, I didn't have the energy to roll over or kick the covers off when it got too hot. My grandmother got on a train in Brooklyn, which was unusual for her, and came to see me in Queens. She sat next to my bed, on a folding chair, and informed me that she finally figured out why she didn't understand my Yiddish. "Because you go to college and you speak a very educated *Eedish.*" If I had had the energy, I would have leapt out of bed and hugged her.

My obsession with the village never diminished. When I went to live in Switzerland, and formed an experimental theatre troupe, I wrote a play about Minkowitz. In experimental performance art, repetition is not necessarily a bad thing, so I used the six facts I knew about Minkowitz over and over; they became a kind of choral refrain and achieved a certain musicality. The audiences were very attentive, and people often told me that they found the play to be unusual and esoteric. I can still hear the echo of one actress intoning, "The floor of the house was made of goat shit," and the chorus repeating, "Goat shit."

My Swiss boyfriend at the time started calling me "Minkowitz" as a term of endearment. "Minkowitz, do you want to go to a movie tonight?" he asked. "Minkowitz, let's go into the country tomorrow."

It seemed pretty normal to me. Why not call me "Minkowitz?" I was obsessed with it by day and dreamed about it at night. It was so vivid and real in my mind that I became convinced I had a past life there.

Growing up, I begged my mother to talk to me about Minkowitz, but she pursed her lips and frowned, as though she had just sucked a lemon. She was born in Brooklyn, she had never been to the village, but certainly she remembered things my grandmother had told her when she was growing up.

"Stop driving me nuts with Minkowitz," she'd say. "They were dirt poor. They didn't have a pot to piss in. Everyone was poor. It was horrible. The Czar's men came in and slaughtered them. That's why they wanted to get away and they don't want to talk about it."

"But, Ma, it's our heritage. I need to know about it."

"How many times do I have to tell you it was awful?"

"Please, I want to know about where I come from and what life was like there."

"It was based on the Jewish calendar. That was what mattered in Minkowitz and all the other dirt-poor *shtetls*, and that was what they brought with them to America."

"So you mean that Grandma was always tuned in to the Jewish calendar?"

"When she lived with us, which is what we did, because we felt responsibility for our parents and didn't send them off to institutions —"

Uh oh. I didn't respond. I didn't feel guilt, sort of. I just waited for her to continue.

"When she lived with us, which of course you don't remember, she would look at the calendar, see which holidays were coming up, and begin to plan for them. Her life was organized, just as it was in the *shtetl*, around the Jewish calendar which included an endless supply of feast days and fast days, in addition to the weekly preparations for Sabbath and the Havdalah ceremony which ended it, after which everyone wished each other a '*guten woch*—a good week.'"

According to my mother, one of the heaviest holidays was Tisha B'av, which commemorates the destruction of the two temples in Jerusalem; although more than 600 years apart, it is said that their demise occurred on the same day of the Jewish calendar. It is also a time to remember other tragedies that befell the Israelites. My mother reported that when she grew up, they ate "*milichdicker*" food on Tisha B'av---dairy only, and no meat. The sadness lasted for nine days, during which time they couldn't swim in the ocean, get married, or celebrate any joyous occasions. My mother emphasized that she and her sister were half-hearted about religious observance, but they did it "because that's the way things were. You respected your parents."

I tried to find out more about my great-grandparents, and, surprisingly, my mother told me that she loved them. When she grew up, she held up a Havdalah candle (a braided candle that is used at the end of Sabbath and certain holidays) and measured it against her grandfather, who was very tall. She wanted her future man to be the same height. Her grandfather was a *melamed*, a learned one, in Minkowitz and when he came to America.

"Wow, ma, I love being descended from a learned man."

"A *melamed* in the *shtetl* was a big nothing. He trained boys for their *bar mitzvah*s, and a *bar mitzvah* was no big deal. They took place on Mondays and Thursdays, and the girls didn't go. They served a piece of herring and some schnapps. That was it."

I tried to picture a little *bar mitzvah* boy and an even littler piece of herring. Truth? Who knows? Anything from the *shtetl* was diminished by my very American mother.

"Please tell me more about this, Ma. Anything you remember of *shtetl* traditions."

"That's it. I'm finished."

"Please. I'm not finished. I have no one else to ask."

"I can't imagine what good it will do you to know this."

"It does me a lot of good. Ma, did they ever tell you what it was like to sail to America in steerage?"

"No."

"They never said anything?"

"I wasn't interested. I never asked. Just count yourself lucky you were born here and not in Minkowitz."

"Ma, I get it. I know how you feel. But I want to understand more about Grandma, and what her life was like before she came here."

"It's of no interest. None."

"Did you ever ask her when you were a child?"

"No. She was a terrible mother to me."

"What did she do?"

"It's what she didn't do. When there was parents' night at school, she never came. She was old school, she spoke Yiddish, she had no interest at all in what I was doing. I came home one day and told her I was the valedictorian. She didn't know if that was a good or bad thing. She said, 'Here, have a glass of milk.' When I was 19, I had a lump on my neck the size of a grapefruit. I had to go to the hospital by myself to have surgery. I could have died, and where was my mother? She was completely, totally, ineffectual. 'Here, have a glass of milk.' That was her response to everything. When I was three years old, I decided to raise myself. Look, I don't want to talk about this."

"It's important to me."

"But it's not important to me. Stop hounding me."

"How did you raise my mother? Was she always difficult like this?" I once asked my grandmother.

"No one could ever tell your mother what to do," she replied, shaking her head sadly. "When she was three years old, she decided

9

to raise herself."

I wanted so badly to have a gentle, caring mother, like the moms I saw on television. But when they were giving out soft mothers, I was at the back of the line. What I had, instead, was a gentle grandmother. My mother was angry and deeply disappointed in her. But I was grateful.

There was nothing exceptional about my grandmother. She wasn't smart, or accomplished. She had a kind of folk wisdom, like the way she talked about fashion. "When your clothes go out of style, you put them in a barrel. When the barrel is full, you turn it over upside down. The clothes that are at the bottom will be back in fashion again."

She was right. Bell-bottoms out, bell-bottoms in. Paisley out, paisley in. Ruffles no. Ruffles yes.

She had a different way of looking at things from my mother, father, sisters, friends, and teachers. Somehow, I believed it was because she was forged in Minkowitz, that mystery place in Russia.

My sisters had no interest in where my grandmother came from. My mother had no interest in where my grandmother came from. I am not even sure my grandmother had any interest in where she came from. But somehow, the finger of fate pointed to me. I was the little flame that burned and burned with curiosity and kept Minkowitz alive.

When my grandmother said, "I love you more than life itself, *mamaleh*," and showed me how to make water bagels by dropping little circles of dough in a pot of boiling water, the way they did it in

Minkowitz, I knew it was my destiny to one day go to Minkowitz and see for myself.

I didn't know where in Russia it was. I didn't know how I would travel there. I didn't know who was left or what language they spoke or what they looked and dressed like. But I knew in my bones that Minkowitz still existed and I vowed to myself that someday I would get there.

The great grandparents from Minkowitz came to America with
suitcases full of superstitions.

CHAPTER TWO -- SUPERSTITIONS AND THE OCCULT

When I was about twelve years old, a button fell off my blouse. I got a needle and some white thread and sat down on the sofa, my back curved into a "c" as I bent forward to reconnect button to blouse. My grandmother walked into the room and, visibly alarmed, told me to quickly stop what I was doing or I would "*fanay* the *sechel*," sew up my brains.

I looked up at my grandmother, trying to understand what she was telling me. I knew I was not skilled as a seamstress, but I could tell the difference between a blouse and my brain.

"*Mamaleh*," she explained, "never, ever, ever, sew anything when you're wearing it. You take it off, and then you sew it. If it's on you, you can sew through your brains."

I would have brushed it off, but because of the seriousness of my grandmother's reaction, I felt a shudder going through me and dropped the needle.

"*Fanaying* the *sechel*" was just one of the superstitions my grandmother brought with her from Minkowitz to the United States. She had learned them from her mother, who later came to the United States and brought her own bundle, which was even bulkier than my grandmother's.

"Ma," I asked my mother, "is it true that you can sew up your brains if you sew clothes that are on your body?"

"Are you kidding? Of course not. It's a *bubba maiseh*, an old wives' tale."

So I had a rational response, my mother's, and a folksy belief, which was my grandmother's. Hedging my bets, I took my blouse off, sewed the button, and never sewed anything on my body again, just in case my grandmother was right.

Most people smile indulgently when they hear about folk beliefs, or else they get annoyed that adults would give any credence to them.

I am not sure how I feel about them. There, I've said it, at the risk of sounding ridiculous. I often wondered how I would fit into life in Minkowitz, where every haystack probably had a superstition attached to it. I know I wouldn't let my life be guided by the beliefs, but I wouldn't ignore them either. Nobody really knows how the world works on an energetic level, or if there are spirits from worlds beyond ours that influence human behavior and outcome. If you step on a crack, does it really break your mother's back? When a black cat passes in front of you, can you be sure it's not an ominous sign? When Phil the groundhog has a long shadow, does it mean there will be a short winter and early spring? Did these superstitions arise out of experience and observation?

How about crossing your fingers or, as I saw in France, holding your thumbs? Full disclosure: I have done the former and thought about doing the latter. In the 5th grade, when I had a crush on a darling, dimpled, green-eyed boy whose forehead was half-obscured by a thick shock of wavy black hair, I snuck outside at midnight and wished upon a star that he would develop a reciprocal crush on me. It was the astrological version of crossing my fingers, and it worked.

"Are horoscopes superstitions?" I asked my mother.

"Of course they are. What person in his right mind would give a crap about whether he was born a Capricorn or a Leo, and then be guided by words in a newspaper that tell him to stay at home or invest in a new venture?"

"So if horoscopes aren't true, why do people read them and believe them?"

"Why do lemmings follow each other and fall of a cliff?"

I became curious about mediums who communicate with other worlds. I wondered if it was possible that an evil *dybbuk* can possess a victim's soul, and that an exorcism must be performed to get rid of it? In Italy, I met a priest who had performed about twenty exorcism rites; he said they were enormously demanding but the success rate was high. I even met a rabbi –of *shtetl* descent– who half-admitted to having excised a *dybbuk*. Both the priest and rabbi were scholarly men. I tried to imagine what an exorcism would look like in Minkowitz, but since I had no idea what the village looked like, it was hard to get past abstractions.

My husband Paul has occasionally expressed exasperation at my superstitions, which he calls "magical thinking." But he also thinks that finding a penny heads up means good luck, or that Chinese fortune cookies may have something going for them. I think he's only half serious about the fortune cookies and pennies, but maybe his other half is serious. After all, his blood, too, comes from the world of the *shtetl*s.

My grandmother would occasionally refer to someone as a *"machashefa,"* or a witch. I thought it was just an expression, but to my grandmother, it was real. A person could masquerade as a human, but really be a witch, which meant she had otherworldly powers, either beneficent or nefarious.

My grandmother's belief in witches inspired me to search the Hebrew Bible, where I learned that Saul, the first king of Israel, banned consulting with witches and trafficking with sorcery in any way, and banished necromancers from Israel. And yet, one night, in the throes of fear and uncertainty about his future at the hands of the Philistines, he disguised himself and snuck off to see the witch of Endor. She called up the spirit of the prophet Samuel, and the news for King Saul wasn't favorable; she predicted he would meet his end violently in battle against the Philistines, and he did.

To this day, I can at least consider that the story may be true.

No matter how much superstitions and occult practices were prohibited and punished in Biblical times, they persisted, even finding their way into the Talmud, the central text of Rabbinic Judaism, where it's revealed that you court bad luck if you find yourself between two dogs or step over water that has been poured. And in normative Judaism, even today, people cast their sins into a moving body of water during a ceremony called Tashlich and, during the Kappores rites, they watch a rabbi swing a live chicken over his head three times to transfer human sins onto the sacrificial fowl. Both rituals are designed to communicate with and propitiate unseen forces and powers. And they're taken very seriously.

Do these things work? If they absolutely did not, why would humans keep doing them for thousands of years and across cultures? The ancients read entrails and consulted with oracles. The moderns carry talismans, wear jewelry that protects them, go to psychics, and don't sign business contracts when Mercury goes retrograde.

I was always intrigued by the occult practices and superstitions that pervaded my ancestors' life in the *shtetl*s. Although the two things are not synonymous, they both involved opening the door to a belief in things beyond the observable material world; and once the portal is open, anything is possible. My grandmother, great grandmother, and all the grandmothers and grandfathers before them practiced superstitious behaviors in an attempt to deal with bad luck, penury, illness, curses, or the prevention of them. When something good happened, they believed that spirits or God had intervened on their behalf. Their neighbors and relatives in the *shtetl* consulted with people who claimed to have direct contact with the world of spirits, and provided answers, solutions, affirmation, or prescribed things to do to bring about or prevent certain occurrences.

In Minkowitz, I learned from my mother, extracting the information the way a dentist extracts a diseased tooth, my great-grandmother was one of these seers, and she looked into balls of melted wax where she had visions of what a person's problem was, and what had to be done to alleviate or remove it. My mother ridiculed the waxy practice, but I am unabashedly proud to be descended from a matriarchal mystic. I'm completely lame in the kitchen, but if I knew how to melt wax and roll it into balls for mystical purposes without ruining a pot, I'd probably be doing it right now.

You could choose to explain everything away by saying that people in the past were beset by poverty, pogroms, lack of good medical care, and great uncertainty. We have science now, but we also have poverty, ethnic cleansing, medical muddles, and great uncertainty. So I think that as long as humans walk the planet, they will reach beyond the material realities of their life and try to curry the favor or solicit the help of unseen forces. My grandmother was one of these people. She was concerned, especially, with the evil eye. As a child, I always thought it was the eyeball of God directing hexes at you, but as an adult, I discovered that the evil eye belongs to the human domain. Other people may be envious of you or wish you ill, and their bad energy is the evil eye. It is so powerful it can harm and even kill you. Children are especially susceptible to the evil eye, and my grandmother frequently said *"kenna hora,"* to keep the evil eye away. She also spat three times—"pooh, pooh, pooh." If she said my sisters and I looked pretty or she praised us, she followed it with *"kenna hora"* and some quick spitting, so as not to elicit envy and bring on the evil eye. And perish the thought you should brag or boast: that was a sure way to evoke the evil eye and bring on bad juju.

My grandmother tied a red string around her children's cribs, which was a deterrent to the evil eye. And she was also concerned with bad energy that came from other realms besides the human.

When my mother, as a child, was sick, my grandmother gave her a new name so it would confuse the Angel of Death and the latter wouldn't find her. Her name was Miriam, and she became Miriam Ruth. During another illness, she became Miriam Ruth Sylvia. Apparently, it worked. My mother survived and thrived.

When my mother reached adulthood, she tried to separate herself from *shtetl* beliefs and put my grandmother's superstitions behind her, but she tied red string on our cribs and had quite a few inherited beliefs that still held sway in her life. She would never get out of bed with the left foot first. Once she left the house, if she forgot something, she wouldn't go back inside. If she walked down the street with someone close to her, she would make sure they were never separated by a telephone pole or street lamp. They both had to walk on the same side of said barrier, or else their relationship would be severed. If someone sneezed while talking, it meant that his or her words were the truth, and that the subject discussed would come to pass.

Fascinated by these beliefs, I asked my mother to tell me more of them. She refused, claiming that she didn't want to foist the superstitions on her children; it was bad enough they had penetrated her own life. The more she withheld, the more I wanted to know.

"I could tell you plenty," she said, "but I won't." And she wouldn't tell me.

This was particularly frustrating to me because of another situation I had with my mother and her refusal to divulge information. When I was growing up, my mother served oatmeal for breakfast, and the glutinous clump in a bowl turned my stomach. I refused to eat it, and she insisted.

"Why don't you eat it?" I asked.

"I could tell you, but I won't," she said.

"Why not?"

"Because. That's all I'll say."

"Because what?"

"Because …it's …a woman thing."

"Tell me."

"You can ask all you want, but I am not going to tell you."

"When will you tell me?"

"When you're old enough."

"How old is that?"

"Thirteen."

During all the intervening years, I croaked down the oatmeal, knowing that one day I would discover a deep, female secret about why my mother didn't eat oatmeal.

The morning of my thirteenth birthday, I bounded into my parents' bedroom and woke my mother up. "I'm thirteen. Now you can tell me why you never ate oatmeal."

"Because I hated it," she said, and then rolled over and went back to sleep. I stood there, consumed with outrage and frustration. Then I began to cackle about how gullible I had been.

I extrapolated from that childhood experience and decided the reason she wouldn't tell me about any more superstitions from the shtetl that had infiltrated her life was because she hated them, the way she hated oatmeal.

I was caught between the pull of my grandmother and the push of my mother. I was a thoroughly modern American, but wherever I went, I had a foot in the Old World. It sought me out and I sought it out. It had nothing to do with my life, and yet it had everything to do with my life.

I am slightly embarrassed to recount how many healers and mystics in the Yucatan, Honduras, Italy, Cambodia, Israel, and countless other countries told me I had to have the evil eye removed. In each case, they removed it, and then gave me something to do as a kind of follow-up when I got home. One gave me a stone, one incense, another a tiny bag with an amulet. I got specific instructions about how to use them, but I never did. I was more interested in the phenomenon of the evil eye than in actually getting it off me. The push and the pull. My grandmother and my mother. The superstitious and the realist. The *shtetl* and the States. I was happy to get the evil eye off me, but I didn't follow through because I wasn't entirely convinced. I lacked the context of the *shtetl*, and I had no way of finding out more than the little I already knew.

I remember vividly an evil-eye-related event that happened to me on the island of Djerba in Tunisia, which is home to what may be the oldest extant Jewish community in the world. Legend traces the Djerba Jews back to the time of King David and King Solomon, about 3,000 years ago. Or perhaps they arrived 2,500 years ago, when the first temple was destroyed in Israel. Or maybe they came after the destruction of the second temple in 70 C.E. It is a deeply mysterious community, where the old men wear black pantaloons with a thin band on the bottom to show mourning for the ancient temple. And they honor, pay homage to, and pray for help and intercession from a woman saint called the Ghriba who lived among them long ago, somewhere back in the mists of time. If she had lived in Djerba instead of Minkowitz, I am sure my grandmother would have been an adept.

Before I left for Tunisia, someone told me about an old woman in the Jewish community who was an expert in dealing with the evil eye, and said I could find her if I asked for her in a shop where they sold *brik*. *Brik*—which has many variants but is traditionally a deep-fried, oil-soaked, triangular-shaped pastry with an egg inside -- is as Tunisian as hamburgers are American so I burst out laughing when I heard that I had to find a *brik* shop. Somehow I found the right one (Intervention of the spirits? Luck? Help from the Ghriba?), and I was guided to an elderly woman who lived with her family in a house that surrounded a central courtyard. In the middle of the central courtyard was a tethered goat.

The old woman hobbled out of her room into the courtyard to meet me and asked why I had come. I replied vaguely that I wanted to experience what she did as a healer. She limped off, gesturing for me to follow her. We went into a back room and she said she needed a piece of my clothes. I was wearing a sky-blue-colored shirt and black tights, so I wasn't sure what to give her. She pointed to my shirt, which I dutifully removed, and for the next twenty minutes I sat in my bra and tights as she manipulated my shirt between her fingers while yawning repeatedly. I was mesmerized by the elasticity of her mouth, which twisted into gargantuan yawns that seemed to grow larger with each inhale.

I wondered if she were really tired, or if I was really boring. I asked a few questions but she didn't answer, as she was tightly focused on my shirt and her yawning. When she finished, she said I had some heavy-duty evil eye energy attacking me, and she had removed it. Her yawning, apparently, disseminated the bad spirits. I don't remember if I felt lighter without the evil eye weighing on me, but I was fascinated, and sorry to leave the woman. I knew I had been privy to something ancient, to ancestral practices that were rapidly vanishing, if they hadn't already disappeared.

When I came back to the U.S., I wished my grandmother were still alive so I could talk to her. Was yawning the equivalent of "pooh, pooh, pooh?" For me, the evil eye was of folkloric interest. For the healer on Djerba island and my grandmother, it was a vital, destructive energy that had to be dealt with and kept at bay.

As for me, once again I was left hanging. I wanted to know the most minute details about the *shtetl*. But my grandmother was gone. My mother, who learned about the superstitions from her mother and grandmother, refused to talk.

Minkowitz was always in my heart, but it was always just beyond my reach. All I had were a handful of superstitions, six facts, and a lot of dead ends.

Minkowitz is a dot on the map in what is, today, Ukraine.

CHAPTER THREE -- A DELI AND A MAP

"Ma," I said one day. "How come you have no interest in Minkowitz?"

"Why would I be interested? I've told you a thousand times. For the thousand and first time, they lived in abject poverty. They couldn't wait to get out of there. It was a miserable life."

"Well, it's about your mother. No matter how you felt about her, aren't you curious about where she came from?"

"Not a bit."

"How can you not be interested? It's your heritage."

"I know plenty about Grandma. I grew up with her. What else do I need to know?"

"I understand how hurt you were as a child and I'm sorry you're still so angry with her."

"I'm not angry. I took my mother in to live with us. I've always taken care of her."

"I know that's true. You certainly did your filial duty. But you're still very angry."

"I am not."

In my general experience, people of my mother's generation are not usually introspective. In my personal experience, there are two ways to have your blood boil: one is to put it in a pan on the stove, and the other is to try to convince my mother of anything.

"Okay. I think I get it, Ma. Because of what your mother didn't do when you were growing up, you didn't care about where she came from. That explains your lack of interest in Minkowitz."

"No it does not. And I don't have to analyze every feeling I have. I'm not interested in Minkowitz because I'm not interested in Minkowitz."

My blood began to simmer. End of grandmother conversation. Time to switch to a deep dialogue about the vagaries of the weather or the correct pronunciation of the word "ascetic."

I had hit a Minkowitz wall with my grandmother and my mother.

Years later, when I lived in Switzerland, a few times a year I took a train to Paris and spent a week or so with a family I knew there. Before returning to Switzerland, I always made a stop in the Marais, the old swamps of Paris, an area that was anything but fashionable then. My destination was Goldenberg's Deli, where I loaded up on bagels, *matza*, gefilte fish and a jar or two of herring.

Once, I was on a train, with two plastic bags emblazoned with the Goldenberg's logo at my side. A burly man with hair the color of a coconut shell and a melon-shaped face sat across from me, staring at the bags.

"*Êtes-vous des nôtres?*" he asked in a thick, guttural accent. "Are you one of us?"

The words made me cringe, as though the world were made up of "us" and "them."

"*Oui*," I said politely. And then, interested in his foreignness, I asked, "Where are you from?"

"Russia."

I leaned forward with conspiratorial intensity.

"My grandmother comes from Russia, but I don't know where her village was."

"What was the name?"

"Minkowitz."

"MINKOWITZ!" he exploded. "I can tell you so many things about Minkowitz."

At that moment, there was a loud whistle and the train squeaked noisily to a halt. The man looked up, and leapt out of his seat.

"This is my stop. I have to get off," he said, and he ran from the train.

I sat there, my mouth hanging open so widely you could have popped an orange into it. I ran over to the window and wrestled it open, hoping the man would call something back to me, leave me with some nugget of information. But he wasn't even visible. I stood there sadly as the train pulled away from the station. Not again, I thought. Another wall. Why do I keep banging into them when it comes to Minkowitz?

One day, a few decades later, when I was living back in the U.S., I was hunched over my computer and got an email offer for five pen pals from five countries for five dollars. I winced. I hardly had enough time to go to the bathroom. Then I thought about it. Maybe it could somehow bring world peace to correspond with folks from other climes. I wrote back, "Yes, I will take you up on this offer, but I need five literate, intelligent people, please."

I was connected to five men. They were literate enough, but four of them were nuts. One referred to women as "harpies," another was oversexed, a third kept asking me if I got turned on by John Dewey, and when I said I was not excited by Dewey decimals, he stopped writing. A fourth compared himself favorably to Alexander the Great. The fifth one, Andrew, was openhearted, bright, and lived in Russia.

By the second exchange of emails, I was grilling him about Minkowitz.

"It's in Ukraine," he wrote. At the time, Ukraine was part of Russia.

"No, I wrote back. My grandmother would have told me if it were in Ukraine. It's in Russia."

"Ukraine," was the terse reply.

And then I didn't hear from Andrew again. I figured I had insulted him, or committed some other e-faux pas.

Several weeks later, a thick envelope arrived. Inside was a huge map of Ukraine with Cyrillic writing. By some coincidence, I had taken three Russian lessons when I was 15, and could decipher the letters. In the southwestern quadrant, there was a circle around a tiny place—Minkivtsi, otherwise known as Minkowitz. Besides the map, Andrew had enclosed an envelope with photos. He had borrowed a car, driven hundreds of miles from L'viv, where he lived, to Minkowitz. I trembled as I opened the envelope to look at my grandmother's dismal homeland. The photos tumbled onto my desk. Minkowitz looked like Switzerland! Rolling hills, animals grazing, sun-dappled fields of green. There were several photos of tombstones, but Andrew apologized that he couldn't decipher the writing. Andrew is Russian Orthodox. The letters were Hebrew.

"I asked the school director if there were any Jews left," Andrew wrote, "and he said there weren't. Just as I was about to leave, an old woman came hobbling up to me. She said the last Jew had left Minkowitz in the 1970's and went somewhere, maybe Israel. The last Jewish person's name was Kornblatt."

Kornblatt!? That was my grandmother's maiden name.

Burial practices from the Old World were transported to America.

CHAPTER FOUR -- THE BURIAL SOCIETY

I called my mother and told her that I had seen Minkowitz on a map and it was in Ukraine.

"It is not," my mother announced.

"But I saw it with my own eyes."

This did not convince my mother, who is smart, funny, well-read, well-informed, and maddeningly rigid and opinionated. When I was growing up in my bibliophilic, semantically supercharged household, I would argue with her about the spelling or pronunciation of a word, and, since she would never back down, I would often go and haul a big dictionary to show her that I was correct. "The dictionary is wrong," she said. How could I argue with that?

"Ma, it's also really beautiful."

"It was a horrible place."

"I saw pictures. I actually saw green, rolling hills that were dappled with sunlight."

"It wasn't Minkowitz."

You may be wondering why I bothered engaging in *shtetl* conversations with my mother, and I wish I had an answer for you. They always ended poorly, yet, after dusting myself off, I went right back into the fray. This is a partial answer: I consider myself to be a rational human being, and I like to assume, even in the face of contradictory evidence, that my mother is too. A darker answer is that children often go back to the parental well even if it is dry. They somehow think, each time, that they will get what they couldn't get before: tenderness, sensitivity, information about Minkowitz. And for another complication, ponder this: Just when I am about to give up my need for satisfaction, when my mother feels that I am squirming on a hook, her maternal instincts rise to the fore and she will, in some way, help me. This time was no exception. And, like all the other times, it convinced me that my mother really was gentle and understanding, until the next time my expectations were dashed.

"If you want more information," she offered, "find out about the Minkowitz burial society. I am sure there is one. When Jews came to this country, one of the first things they did was form a burial society."

My mother was right. And it wasn't only Jews who wanted to ensure that their bodies were buried in the right place and they would have family and spouses around them for life's final passage. The tradition of burial societies actually goes back to ancient Greece and Rome, and perhaps even before that. People belonged to different trade, political, and religious groups and they paid monthly dues so that when they died, the association would provide them with proper funeral rites and a burial.

In the early twentieth century, when there was a mass exodus of Eastern European Jews to America, many thousands of Jewish *landsmanshaftn*, or social organizations, sprung up. Members usually came from the same village or city and helped each other with financial and medical needs, including the need to have and maintain burial plots. Over time, the other functions sometimes faded, but the importance of burial societies persisted, especially in the northeast. Like the Greeks and Romans, these immigrants were very concerned with where their bodies would be put to rest; they wanted to be near their loved ones for all eternity. They paid regular dues to the societies to ensure maintenance of the plots and burial fees. Their meetings were a time to socialize and schmooze. Of course, they discussed financial matters and maintenance issues, but I imagine that news, gossip and bonding—issues of life, rather than death— were as important as practical, burial-related matters.

It took me a while to get information about the Minkowitz burial society. I called cemeteries and organizations and one person referred me to the next. Just as I was about to give up, a woman told me that she knew about the Minkowitz society: there were only two elderly members left, and they were brothers. Another gaggle of calls, and I found their names and phone numbers.

I was worried that the two calls I was about to make would be the end of the line for me as I had run out of ideas for finding out more about Minkowitz. Andrew's map indicated that the *shtetl* was in Ukraine, but my mother had sown seeds of doubt that sprouted in my brain.

I dialed the number of the first brother very slowly. "Please let him tell me what I want to know," I intoned. I am not sure to whom I addressed the prayer. Maybe to the Cosmic *Shtetl* Locator.

A man picked up the phone with a brusque, "Yes?"

I talked very fast, telling him that my grandmother came from Minkowitz, that I had been trying to track the village down all of my life, and I said I would be very grateful if he would share memories and information with me.

I was completely unprepared for what happened next. The man unleashed a volley of curses and insults and when I interrupted for a moment to ask what I had done wrong, he got louder and louder until he was screaming at me and damning me and everyone I knew for all eternity.

I hung up the phone, shocked. At that moment, I had two choices: I could give up or call the second brother, and risk damnation for a second time in one day. My fingers started punching the keypad.

A man answered the phone and asked why I was calling. I went through an abbreviated explanation and, at the end, tagged on the fact that his brother had skewered me and consigned me to hell.

"I am sorry about my brother," he said. "He suffers from dementia. I, myself, am quite old, and have been sick lately. I am happy to talk to you, but I tire easily, so it can't be for long."

Oh my God, I thought. There is a jackpot. I have just hit it.

I expressed sincere, profuse gratefulness and asked the man if his village was in Ukraine.

"Today it is," he said.

Yes!!

"Can you tell me where it is located?" I asked.

"Ushitsa," he said.

Oh, no, I was being cursed again. First I was the consort of the devil, and now I was shit.

"I shit?" I asked, a bit squeamishly.

"No, no, the name of the river is Ushitsa," he explained.

This could only happen to me, I thought.

"I am very tired now. I hope I have helped you," the man said.

I blessed him, wished him good health, thanked him from the bottom of my obsessed heart, hung up the phone, went back to Andrew's map, and there, indeed, running through the dot that was Minkowitz, was the river Ushitsa.

I now knew that I came from Ukraine, and I could go to visit my grandmother's birthplace.

Yet, for some reason which I couldn't understand, even if I had been analyzed by a team that consisted of Freud, Jung, Milton Erikson, Fritz Perls and Alfred Adler, I didn't jump on a plane and fly to Ukraine so I could finally go to Minkowitz.

I am a travel journalist. I go all over the world. But for twenty years I couldn't get to Minkowitz, even though I knew where it was.

"I guess you aren't ready," Paul said.

"I guess you are right."

The young married couple does a voice-over for their wedding.

CHAPTER FIVE -- MARRIED WITH SPOON

Whenever I listened to friends talk about their romantic relationships, and whenever I fretted about my own, I always thought to myself: when it's right, it's easy.

It couldn't have been easier with Paul Ross. We met, we laughed, I served him thrice-reheated turkey that set off the fire alarm and freshly-washed lettuce that dripped through a colander onto his lap. "I don't care if you can't boil an egg or drop a slice of bread into a toaster," he said. He liked cooking. I broke out in hives when I had to enter the kitchen. It was perfection. Soon we were living together. And two years later, it occurred to me that it might be sweet to be married, even though the woman who thought of pairing Paul and me had said, "He's not the marrying kind."

A few days later, adorned in a t-shirt, underwear and socks, which was my usual Hollywood screenwriter's garb, I sat on the sofa, talking on the phone to a director with whom I was working. It was an intense discussion about some project or other, and he was giving me script notes while Paul bounded into the apartment, proffering a little jewelry box. I held up an index finger, indicating that he should wait a minute.

He waited, and the phone conversation went on. And on.

Finally, Paul opened the little box and showed me a divine wedding ring set: two graceful gold bands that were dotted with diamonds.

Still, I talked on the phone, hanging on the words of a director who behaved as though he were a demi-god, but he was actually a hopeless narcissist and egomaniac.

Finally, Paul dropped to his knees. I knew it was time to get off the phone.

"I love you. Will you marry me?" Paul asked, balancing on his patella.

I was the one who wanted to get married, but when he popped the question, I froze in terror. I'd already had one disastrous marriage and wasn't ready to leap into the maw of another, just in case it turned sour.

"Uh.....thank you. Let me think about it. I'll get back to you."

"Well," said Paul, in fine Hollywood fashion, "you'd better give me an answer soon or I'll pitch it elsewhere."

Two fraught weeks later, I accepted. I called my mother and Paul called his parents, about whom I have something significant to relate.

When Paul and I first started dating, laughing and meshing for several months, he thought it might be a good idea for me to meet his folks. The date was set, and the locus was selected: a Chinese restaurant.

When I walked in, I flashed my widest smile, and walked right over to Paul's progenitors. His mother's opening line to me, after looking at my pearly whites and the small gap between the two front ones, was: "You know, dear, even adults can get that space closed up."

I held out my hand to his father, who took it and said, "Nice hands. How are your buns?"

Oh my God. Where could the conversation go from there? We sat down, ordered our food, and I tried desperately to make a verbal connection.

"Where are you originally from?" I asked.

"Philly," said his father.

"New York," replied his mother, with an affected British accent.

I wondered what to ask next. "Uh...where do your parents come from?"

Paul's father volunteered that his hailed from a small *shtetl* in Russia.

"What's the name?" I inquired.

"Minkowitz."

And with that, I fell off my chair, clutching a pair of chopsticks and a crisp, vegetable egg roll. How was it possible that our ancestors came from the same remote speck on the map?

I asked the head of the University of Judaism if he had ever heard of such a thing. He said no, frankly, he never had.

And then I noticed something uncanny. When Paul and I walked around Santa Monica, which we often did, children sometimes stopped us in the street and asked if we were related. Mutual friends said we looked alike. I reflected that the gene pool in the *shtetl*s was pretty restricted. The *shtetl*-dwellers married their own. Was it possible that we were actually kin?

"Probably," Paul mused. "If we ever had kids, there would be something wrong with them... like they'd be politicians."

We began to work up a little routine about our past life together in Minkowitz. We both affected the Yiddish accents of our grandparents. Paul talked about his putative life in the *shtetl*, "ver der vas one chicken, and I vas a chicken plucker for special holidays. At other times, I vas a raisin sorter, or I sold icon cleaner, door to door." We howled every time we did our Minkowitz shtick.

When Paul told his parents we were getting married, his father offered us something very meaningful and personal: the only thing left from the *shtetl*. It was a soup spoon that his parents brought with them as they sailed in steerage from the Old Country to America. I held it, patted it gently, and treasured it because it made our ancient connection so real to me.

My mother refused to come to the wedding because I told her there was not going to be a rabbi. "I don't care how and I don't care when, I just care *who*."

"Ma, it's our wedding. We're not observant. We don't need a rabbi."

"And then you don't need me. No rabbi, no mother. I will not come."

"Ma, I don't have a father anymore. How can I have a wedding without my mother?"

She held her ground for about two weeks, refusing to attend

unless I agreed to hire a rabbi. Finally, Paul picked up the phone and screamed at her to stop laying her controlling crap on me. No one outside of our family had ever yelled at my mother. From then on, she retreated from Paul, and held onto her resentment of him for decades.

The wedding day came. We got married in the Variety Arts Center in downtown Los Angeles. The location was seedy, but the building was fabulous; a museum of performing arts, including Ed Wynn's bicycle-piano combination, vaudeville sets, recordings of Al Jolson, and props.

Paul and I were about to cross the street to the Variety Arts building, and I had my wedding gown draped over my arm. As we waited for the light to change, a down-on-his luck drunk who was camped out on the ground, marinating in his own bodily fluids, stood up and reeled towards me. I looked him in the eyes as he gave me this marital advice in a gravelly baritone: "If you love him, get off his ass."

"Truer words were never spoken," Paul commented, as the man careened away.

We had planned a Variety Arts wedding—with performances by an opera singer, mimes, a monologist—and we got married on the set of the old *Tonight Show* where Johnny Carson captivated a late-night nation. Just before the actual ceremony started, we played a voice-over tape we had prepared beforehand; it sounded as though it was being piped in from our dressing room, and the guests were able to hear what was going on. I kept urging Paul to stop working and get dressed. I reminded him that it was our wedding day. Apparently, the guests fell for it and believed we had accidentally left a microphone on.

We had arranged that I was to walk onto the *Tonight Show* set and wait for Paul, who made his entry from the old fire escape. We didn't count on it raining. Paul almost slipped to his death on the ladder, and then slid into his own wedding, skidding to a halt in front of his bride.

There were a few glitches on our wedding day. First, let me admit that I yielded to maternal pressure and we got a rabbi, but he was not your average religious leader. He had his congregation chant and intone "Shal---ohmmmmm" and he was more mystical than ministerial.

Jewish weddings take place under a canopy, called a *chupa*, and ours was no exception. It is a great honor to hold one of the four corners of a *chupa* for a couple during the ceremony, and we asked our parents to do it. My mother was wearing a huge, glitzy ring on her index finger. "Rabbi," she bellowed in her dulcet New York tones, "I want to stand where I can show off my *chupa* ring!" As for Paul's parents, they declined. Paul's mother said she didn't want people looking at her. We explained that normally people at a wedding look at the bride and groom rather than the groom's mother, but she refused to hold up the canopy. We were caught between a rock star mother and my hard place mother-in-law.

The ceremony started, and I have only two distinct memories of it: We recited our own wacky vows, and we made a place of honor under the *chupa*, on a satin pillow, for the spoon from Minkowitz.

"What's the spoon for?" my mother whispered. "Are you using it for cough syrup?"

As soon as the ceremony was over, Paul's parents put on their coats and came to say goodbye. Goodbye? The wedding reception hadn't even begun.

"Well, dears," said his mother in her finest faux-British accent, "We have tickets for the ballet." And they left. Really. Hey, we knew how expensive season tickets were.

It was hurtful and crazy, but Paul's dad had nonetheless made a vital contribution to the nuptials: the Minkowitz spoon.

CHAPTER SIX -- THE LIGHT OF THE WORLD-TO-COME

Paul and I had been working non-stop for several months, and it was either take a break, or be broken. We flew to lush, tropical Kauai, checked into a resort, donned our bathing suits, ran into the warm water, ate a whole pineapple, hung a "Do Not Disturb" sign on the door handle of our room, and crashed. No one knew where we were.

Then the phone rang. I looked quizzically at Paul. Who could be calling? It must be a wrong number. The phone rang insistently. I picked it up. It was a woman who went to Junior High School with me. I hadn't heard from her in 20 years.

"Diane, how in the world did you track me down?"

Diane is very mysterious. She didn't answer.

"No one in the world knows we are here. "

Silence.

"Diane, this is really odd."

"I am calling to tell you that I have free phone calls to anywhere in the world for a few days. I thought you might want to take advantage of it."

This was pre-international calling plans, pre-inexpensive calling cards -- prefrontal cortex, as far as I was concerned. How did Diane choose me?

"Is there someone you want to speak to?" she asked.

"I'm in Kauai. I don't want to speak to anyone. I just want to shut up, swim, walk, and....wait a minute. There is someone I need to talk to: my grandmother."

"I thought so," Diane said enigmatically.

She placed a call to the retirement home in Far Rockaway. No one answered in my grandmother's room. She called again. Still no answer. Then she rang the desk and after I identified myself, I was informed that my grandmother was in the hospital. Diane immediately dialed the hospital and was connected to my grandmother's room. The phone rang about 10 times.

I paced back and forth, in an agitated state. Diane was about to hang up when my mother answered the phone.

"Ma, how is Grandma?"

"Horrible. She's in terrible pain. They can't relieve it. It's her heart. She's not going to make it. I knew it was going to be awful the minute I arrived."

I fell backwards into a chair, as though someone had punched me.

"I have to get off now. I can't talk anymore," my mother insisted.

"Ma, let me speak to Grandma."

"Are you crazy? She's completely out of it. She can't talk. I don't even know if she's aware I'm here."

"Ma, please."

"I'm hanging up now."

"Ma….."

The phone went dead.

I started babbling to Paul that I didn't know what to do. I wanted to talk to my grandmother. My mother wouldn't let me. I didn't want my grandmother to die. And I didn't want her to go without talking to her. Forget relaxing on Kauai. I flopped around all night like a beached fish, and when I dozed off for a few minutes, I had menacing dreams, so I decided to stay awake.

I wondered what my grandmother was feeling in her hospital bed. Emotionally, she was lucky, because, having been raised in a *shtetl*, she inherited and was exposed to a worldview that was logical and orderly. When something good happened, she thanked God. When something bad happened, she grieved, but accepted that it was God's will.

When my grandmother referred to a deceased person, she always added, "May his soul rest in peace." When my father died, she donated a silver Torah pointer – designed to keep one's place when reading from the holy book – to her synagogue. Somehow, saying the right words or offering a gift to God and His house of worship made the pain a little less searing. It was something one could do, instead of being completely overwhelmed by misery. And every year, on the day of a family member's death, a *yahrzeit* candle was lit; it burned for 24 hours. It kept the memory of the departed person alive, and I always thought it was an annual connection, a bridge between the living and the dead.

My grandmother accepted that in this world, there was

suffering, loss, torment. But in the *Olam Haba*, the next life, the world-to-come, it would be better.

Early the next morning, Diane called.

"Let's try again," she said.

The phone in my grandmother's room rang and rang, and finally my mother picked it up.

"I can't stand it," she said, in obvious pain and with empathy for my grandmother. "She's suffering so badly."

"Ma, let me speak to Grandma."

"No."

"Please. I'm asking you to let me talk to her."

"You're so removed from reality. She doesn't know what is going on and she can't speak."

"Ma, can you please hold up the phone to her ear?"

"Stop being crazy."

"LISTEN. I AM NOT ASKING YOU TO FLY ME TO JUPITER. JUST HOLD THE PHONE UP TO HER EAR SO I CAN TALK TO HER."

"I'm getting off now. The nurse is here."

I was gnashing my teeth. Then my jaw locked. My heart was racing. The hand that held the phone was drenched in sweat. Talking to my mother was like trying to bend concrete.

"ASK THE NURSE TO HOLD THE PHONE UP TO HER EAR. I NEED TO TALK TO HER."

The nurse did what my mother wouldn't. I thanked her profusely. And then I spoke to my grandmother. I became very focused and still inside. It didn't matter what fear or sadness or frustration I was feeling. This was about my grandmother, and not about me.

"Grandma, do you know who this is?"

I heard a low grunt that sounded like yes.

"It's me. Judie. Grandma, are you in pain?

Another affirmative grunt.

"Grandma, are you afraid to die?"

I heard a weak no.

"Are you ready to die, to go to the *Olam Haba*?"

An even weaker "yes."

"Do you know how to die?"

A barely discernible "no."

There was nothing else in the world at that moment except a straight, taut line that connected me to my grandmother. There was no past, no present, no one else in the hotel room where I stood or the room where my grandmother lay dying.

"Gram, very soon you are going to see all the people you have lost. And you will be in a realm of beautiful, beautiful light. I know you are tired. Very tired. I will stay with you now. All you have to do is walk toward the light. Gram, it's a gentle walk to the *Olam Haba*. Just move towards the light. You can walk now, Gram."

Someone took the phone from my grandmother's ear, I heard my mother talking to the nurse, muffled noises, and then somebody hung up the phone.

Twenty minutes later, my grandmother's soul left her body.

My mother and sisters denied the timeline and that I had spoken to my grandmother, but I didn't care. I knew what the truth was. My grandmother had given me her most precious gift before leaving: She allowed me to be with her before she walked into the light of the *Olam Haba.*

I would never again hear her say, "*Mamaleh,* I love you more than life," or "I'm singing and dancing." I could never ask her another question, or feel her soft skin. There would be no more calls to the home in Far Rockaway. There was no more living connection to Minkowitz.

Grandma was dead. She was part of the *Olam Haba.* May her soul rest in peace.

CHAPTER SEVEN -- FOREPLAY TO MINKOWITZ

I f you pinned me to a wall and threatened to cut off my Internet access, I still couldn't tell you why I never went to Minkowitz. Perhaps it had become a habit—thinking about the *shtetl* and then resigning myself to the fact that it would only live in my imagination because I would never go there. I couldn't figure out who would take me to Minkowitz, arrange for transportation, act as a translator, navigate the world of the *shtetl*s, make hotel reservations, find restaurants. Even though I consider myself a resourceful world traveler and travel journalist, it seemed daunting. I was in a rut, a no-Minkowitz zone.

And then, just when I had given up, a concatenation of events pushed me closer than ever to Minkowitz and Ukraine. It began when I was walking in the hills around Santa Fe with a new friend, and we discovered we had both gone to the same university, both worked as Hollywood screenwriters, and were both interested in the *shtetl*s where our ancestors once lived. I told her about my Minkowitz obsession, and she sighed and said that she had hit a wall and couldn't get any information on her family *shtetl* on Jewish Gen.

"What's Jewish Gen?" I asked.

She said it was Ground Zero for *shtetl* research. You go to JewishGen.org, plug in the name of a *shtetl* or an ancestor's name and suddenly you are tapped into a world of information.

The minute our walk was over, I ran to my computer and typed in the URL. The site came up, and I entered Minkowitz and my grandmother's name. Within a minute or two, I found a list of people who had an ancestral link to Minkowitz and environs. Lunchtime passed. I forgot to eat. For the first time in my life, I missed appointments I had made and conference calls I had set up. I was busy emailing people with a Minkowitz connection or a connection to nearby areas of Ukraine, reading what they wrote, learning what they knew about their family *shtetl*s.

A day later, Paul and I decided to sign up for a Viking River Cruise to the Waterways of the Czars in Russia. When we looked at a map, we saw that Ukraine was an inch away from the final port. "Paul?" I asked. "Minkowitz," he replied.

I was feverish. I tracked down a Yale law professor named Eugene who had a book about Kamenetz Podolsk and environs. When I couldn't find a copy, he offered to send me his, on loan.

I wrote to my pen pal Andrew and asked him which airport we should fly into if we wanted to be close to Minkowitz. He wrote back immediately, insisting that if we travel to Ukraine, we should fly to L'viv and stay at his house for as long as we wished.

I was sleeping four hours a night, four restless, agitated hours. I got up at 3 a.m. to research guides. When someone mentioned Alex Denisenko, I wrote to him, and discovered that he was available. He suggested an itinerary, which, truth be told, I never read. I answered every email with the same refrain: "I want to explore the environs, but the heart of my trip is Minkowitz. I want to spend as much time there as possible."

There was a flurry of emails back and forth. What quality of hotel did I want? I wrote that as long as it was comfortable and clean, I didn't care. Alex said he would be the guide and translator, and he'd hire a car and driver to get us around. Fine. It would cost a fair amount of money because we had to pay for hotel and food for the guide and driver, and expenses for the car. Fine. I didn't care if I had to stand on my head and whistle the theme song from the film _Yentl_. After a lifetime of fruitless searching and longing, I was going to Minkowitz. Paul was amenable to whatever I decided to do. He was interested. I was obsessed.

In every email, I reminded Alex that the heart of the trip was Minkowitz. Other than that, I was open to any of his suggestions, as I wanted to find out about the world my grandmother came from, and to see what was left of *shtetl* life. "I want to know if the Fiddler is still on the Roof," I wrote, "or if he has packed up his fiddle because the roof was demolished. So we can go anywhere, as long as we end up in Minkowitz."

Alex sent me the names and highlights of towns in Ukraine, but I glazed over when I read them. You'd think that as a travel writer and Minkowitz obsessive, I would have parsed every word and googled my fingers off. But I didn't. I want to be Marco Polo. When I travel somewhere, I want to encounter a world I know nothing about. I want to feel as though I am the first person who ever traveled there. I want to use all my mental, emotional, and physical resources to get underneath the surface. I want to revel in discovery, uncovering aspects of a place that are meaningful and moving. I want to be surprised, delighted, entranced, instructed. In short, I want something unexpected to happen. If I read about and study places before I go there, I am influenced by guidebooks and trip advisories, and my experience will be like coffee grounds that have already gone through someone else's filter.

So I automatically said yes to most of the places Alex suggested, without really knowing anything about them.

About a month before the trip to Russia and Ukraine, Paul and I were having dinner with a group of friends in an Asian fusion restaurant. Over stuffed lettuce cups and crisp tempura, we laughed and joked and then they asked the question people always ask us: "Where are you going next?" Actually, it was a question that irritated me. We are hardly off the plane from Vanuatau or Lapland, and people ask: "So where's your next trip?" "What do you mean, 'next trip?'" I feel like saying. "We just got back. We haven't even unpacked. We've schlepped halfway around the world, and all you can ask is where we are going next?"

This time the question didn't annoy me, because the upcoming trip had been in the planning stages since my prepubescent days. I mentioned that I was going to my grandmother's village, and I quickly became so passionate and emotional that people were turning around from adjacent tables to stare at me. "In a month, I am going to track down my grandmother's village," I said, with great intensity. "I only have six clues about it, six little factoids that I have clung to all my life. I am absolutely determined to find it because that is where I come from. And not only do I come from there, but Paul does too."

They all turned to look at Paul. He nodded enthusiastically as he swallowed a spoonful of Thai soup.

"My conviction is this," I continued. "We can't know who we are unless we know where we came from. An apple doesn't come from nowhere. A lion was born from a lioness who came from a lioness before her."

There was radio silence at the table. Even the waitperson stood there without speaking.

"Do you all know where your ancestors come from?" I asked.

None of them did. One knew the name of a town, but had never looked for it on a map. The others knew which country, but little more. Another knew nothing at all.

"There were people who came before us," I said. "We owe it to them to find out who they were, how they lived."

Once again, total silence at the table. I thought it was a lack of interest, but it turned out to be a long moment of introspection for my friends. They expressed their longing to know about their ancestors, even though most of them were gone and it was too late. They expressed regrets that they had never asked. Or that they had asked, and never been told.

"Tell me how it is when you have come back," a woman said.

The others all echoed the sentiment. They wanted to know what I found, and if anything was left. They wanted to hear if I was disappointed, moved, changed by what I encountered. They were curious about my ancestor, and, I realized, curious about their own.

A week before the trip, I began to have difficulty sleeping. I lay in bed every night, going over the six facts my grandmother had given me when I was a young child, and to which I had clung all of my life. There was a market on Tuesdays. My grandmother sat with the women, drying tobacco leaves. She lived at the bottom of a hill. The Russian girls went to school on top of the hill. The floor of the house was made of goat shit. Kamenetz Podolsk was the largest town in the area.

My mother and sisters thought it was dumb to go halfway around the world to a village none of them cared about, tracking my grandmother, who was inconsequential to them. I didn't bother arguing with them. Let them keep their beliefs that ancestry didn't matter, and I would keep mine, that it mattered deeply. For them, what preceded our lives in America was over and gone. For me, there was a long finger that beckoned from across the ocean, across space and time.

I emailed Alex to firm up the arrangements. I sent flight information and arrival time in L'viv to Andrew. I told everyone I knew that I was going on a very different kind of trip, a trip back through time, to where I came from, and I promised to tell them what I found.

I never expressed to anyone my deepest fear: that I would find nothing at all, that the world my grandmother left behind was gone, replaced by apartment buildings, chain supermarkets, and fast food eateries selling burgers on buns.

And then an awful thing happened. Paul's cousin emailed him

and said he didn't come from Minkowitz. His ancestors came from a place called Tushinov. Paul and I totally freaked.

"Is there anyone still alive you can call and ask?"

Paul shook his head no.

"Please, Paul, write to your cousin. Ask her if there is anyone still alive. Please."

Paul did, and he found the name of an elderly aunt. He wasn't even sure if she was an aunt. He didn't know how the aunt was related to his father. He didn't want to call. He was confused, befuddled. Finally, just before the zero hour of departure, he dialed the number. The conversation was short. He was expressionless.

"Well…?"

"It wasn't a very useful call. I guess she's pretty old and the answers weren't clear."

"Paul, was it Tushinov or Minkowitz?"

"I don't know."

"If it wasn't Minkowitz, how did your father know the name of the town? Maybe he was born in Tushinov and then moved to Minkowitz?"

Paul didn't reply for a long while. When he did, he simply said, "I have decided it is Minkowitz. It's our place. Our life together. That's what matters. We're going to where we both came from."

The day of our departure arrived. Paul loaded up the car, and we drove to the airport. First stop: Russia. Second stop: the land of my ancestors, Paul's ancestors, and the *shtetl* of my heart, Minkowitz.

The author and pen pal Andrew at a market in L'viv.

CHAPTER EIGHT -- FACE TIME WITH ANDREW

It's very odd to have a pen pal for 20 years without ever having seen a photo of him. I was indebted to Andrew for telling me that Minkowitz was in Ukraine, for sending photos, for undertaking the trip to my grandmother's *shtetl* two decades ago, and for insisting that I stay in his house if I ever came to Ukraine. Although we had never met, he was an actor in my life story, and I wanted to find a way to thank him.

"Andrew," I wrote in an email, "I want to bring you something special. Please, please, tell me what you would like."

"Nothing," he wrote back.

"How about something unique from one of the countries we have visited? Would that please you?"

"Don't bother. It will just end up in the attic."

"Clothes?"

"No."

"Electronics?"

"I have everything I need."

"Andrew, I am begging you. We will not arrive empty-handed. There must be something in the world that would give you pleasure."

"Nothing. Nothing."

"You are making me miserable. Let me off the hook. Name something."

"If you absolutely insist, then there are a few jazz albums I am missing."

We bought the CD's and some ethnic jewelry for Andrew's wife. The email exchange about the gifts reinforced the image I had of Andrew in my mind: He was a tech guy, and was probably slight, bespectacled, emotionally reigned-in, ascetic, and exceedingly cerebral.

When Paul and I got off the plane in L'viv, my upper and lower lips parted in surprise. The tall, burly, vigorous, buoyant man holding a large photo of me, which he had downloaded from the Internet, was everything I didn't imagine him to be: expressive, openhearted, and as gentle, warm and cuddly as a stuffed animal from childhood.

"I can't believe it's you!" I said.

"And I can't believe it's you," he echoed.

"You're so tall!" I exclaimed.

"You're so short," he countered.

"You're so different from your emails!"

"Well, it's not my language . . ."

And then we stopped making small talk and began to hug. We held onto each other as though we were long-lost classmates or cousins who were headed to a family reunion. He was well dressed in a Casual Friday kind of way, and took one of our carry-on bags in each hand as he escorted us to his expensive, late-model SUV.

"Andrew," I said, as we got into the car," I feel as though I am in a dream. All my life I have wanted to be here. And you've helped me to make it real."

"There is something I must tell you," he said. "Twenty years ago I was in Minkowitz and although I don't remember it exactly, I am afraid you are going to be disappointed. It is a modern town in Ukraine now."

I put my hand over my heart to shelter it from the wave of sadness that washed over me.

"You mean apartment buildings and shops?"

He nodded.

"Cars and concrete buildings?"

He nodded again.

I didn't want to believe him. "I am sure that there are still pockets of history."

"I don't think so."

I retreated into myself and began to panic. What was I doing in Ukraine? Why didn't I listen to everyone who warned me that the world of my grandmother was gone? Maybe my mother and sister were right. Why was I so damn stubborn? The intense dream I started dreaming in childhood started to unravel and disintegrate. I covered my mouth with my hand, so I wouldn't make sobbing, anguished noises. It was all disappearing before my eyes – Minkowitz – the spoon we used at our wedding, the joy, the excitement I had carried with me for as long as I could remember. What did I think I was connected to? It was a fantasy, an illusion, a delusion.

Paul understood what I was feeling. He put his arm around me and drew me close to him. I leaned against him for support and comfort.

"Come on," Andrew said, interrupting my downward spiral. "Let me show you both some special things in L'viv."

We drove through the historic downtown with its opera house, town hall, churches, restaurants, hotels, and Renaissance buildings. They were beautiful, but they were a blur to me. I didn't come for beauty. I wanted connection. I didn't want to just see. I wanted to feel. I wasn't interested in the present. I wasn't a tourist. I wanted to slip through the cracks or down a rabbit hole and find myself in the world my grandmother left behind.

We stopped at a huge, sprawling market near the railway station. Andrew led us past stalls with wonderfully abundant produce: mushrooms, cauliflower, sausages, potatoes, strawberries, cherries, beets, peppers, spices, fish, meat, clothes, handmade brooms, embroidery. I waved at vendors, and expressed my pleasure at seeing how fertile and bountiful Ukraine was, but inside I was still caught in the web of deep, personal disappointment, unable to extricate myself.

Then, off to the side, I saw a woman in a timeworn, dark green suit with a printed white babushka, selling milk in a large plastic water bottle with a bright green cap. In an instant, modern L'viv dissolved in front of my eyes, and I saw Minkowitz.

"Please, Andrew, can you translate if I speak to her?" I implored.

He seemed surprised by my request, but obliged. It turned out that the woman traveled 50 kilometers (about 30 miles) by train to come to the market. She possessed one cow that provided about four liters of milk a day, which she poured into plastic bottles. At the market, she could sell the milk for four or five dollars, and then make the 50-kilometer trip back home with her meager earnings.

"The train ride is free," Andrew translated, "because she is a pensioner."

"Blessings to you, blessings," I whispered to the woman.

She raised her eyes and looked at me.

'Thank you," I said in Russian, hoping she would understand.

I walked over to Paul, and grabbed his arm.

"Minkowitz?" he asked, with a grin.

"Minkowitz," I replied. "Please, Paul, ask the woman if you can photograph her."

"It's already done," he said.

We walked about twenty feet and saw an elderly vendor, who wore a dark green vest over a bulky, beige sweater, a white floral babushka, a dark blue skirt, gray leggings, and what seemed to be men's black boots. She had empty spaces in her mouth where teeth had once been, and sat on an old backless chair. Woven nylon shopping bags were piled up near her feet. She introduced herself as Nadia, and said she was 90 years old and hailed from Chernobyl. Before I could ask about the nuclear disaster, she explained that she was evacuated three or four days after the explosion in 1981, and given a compensatory payment of 12,000 rubles—which was a lot of money. Roughly equivalent to $4,000 dollars, enough to buy a major purchase like a car. The money was put in a Soviet bank, but after the unexpected breakup of the Soviet Union, the money became worthless and she lost everything. In order to survive, she came to the market to sell flower bulbs and other odds and ends, like a brightly colored soccer ball.

"I got it from collecting the Marlboro logo from cigarette packages," Nadia told us. "I send them in, and I get a gift—like the soccer ball—that I can sell at the market."

She opened a nylon bag and showed us a gaggle of bottle caps, which she was going to mail in to claim a gift that could be sold. She said her husband had died at age 52 when he was in the army, and she never remarried. When she left Chernobyl, she moved in with her daughter in L'viv.

As Andrew translated Nadia's narrative, I clung to every word. I stood very close to her and we locked eyes.

"Does this really interest you?" Andrew asked incredulously.

"You have no idea," I answered. "You live in a vibrant, contemporary city, but these women take me back . . . to the world my grandmother came from. I am sure my great-grandmother looked just like Nadia, and had the kinds of struggles Nadia has. It's all here, Andrew, right here in the middle of L'viv. Rural poverty. Eking out a living. Women who are resourceful. Courageous. Wearing *babushkas*. You opened a door to the past for me, and I walked inside."

Before I could finish explaining, Nadia reached out to me, and pulled me close to her. We embraced and held onto each other. I didn't want to leave the market. Andrew fiddled with his keys.

"Goodbye, dear Nadia," I whispered. "Thank you." She didn't understand my words, but she nodded, understanding my feelings.

Andrew drove us back to his house to meet his wife Oksana, who, unlike Andrew, didn't like traveling, exploring the city or even going far from her house. She worked at home, sewing elegant and princely vestments for priests, and spent her spare time taking care of her grandchildren while her son and daughter-in-law worked. Andrew was an extrovert and Oksana was a homebody and a nurturer. When it was chilly, she threw a sweater over my shoulders. On the pillows of the guest bed, she draped silk bathrobes for Paul and me. Over the course of our stay, she whipped out Ukrainian delicacies and showered us with gifts, hospitality, and arguably the world's best *borscht* (beet soup).

"*Borscht*," I intoned. "The nectar my grandmother drank."

Andrew looked up the word "nectar" in a dictionary and translated it to Oksana. "*Borscht* is nectar?" she asked quizzically. I am sure she thought I was nuts.

The following day, Andrew took us for a ride in the countryside north of L'viv. Everywhere we looked were expansive farms, people working in fields, verdant pastures, red wild flowers, brick and cement houses, cows, horses, and cowherds dressed in jeans. A sign on the side of the road announced "Lublin, Poland, 40 kilometers." My mind was ablaze with the Isaac Bashevis Singer novel, *The Magician of Lublin*, about *shtetl* life in the late 1800's. Andrew was perplexed at why a road sign would excite me, but anything that harkened back to the world and time of my grandmother inflamed my soul. I didn't just want to absorb everything; I *needed* to. I felt as though my life—or at least my identity—depended on it. It was as though I was on a mission assigned to me in childhood, and the most important job in my life was to fulfill it.

We drove to the small town of Zhoukva, which was established in 1368. In the historic center, a local man pointed out a wooden church from 1720. It was hewn from huge logs interspersed with sheep wool. Further on, we entered a seventeenth-century church adorned with magnificent frescoes, icons, and pictures framed by Ukrainian embroidery.

"Peter the Great lived there," another local man told us as we walked by the castle. "See that pink house? He resided there for six months during the Swedish war and addressed people from the balcony."

Because we were the only tourists in town, a government-sponsored guide spotted us and offered to show us around. I smiled, shook her hand, and my Minkowitz story came pouring out of my mouth.

"Then I think I will take you to see our very important synagogue. It dates to two hundred years before your grandmother's time. Are you interested?"

I burst out laughing. I would have been intrigued if she had held up a moth-eaten pair of socks from my grandmother's world.

"Good. I believe if we go there it will give you some insight into how rich and influential the Jews were in this small town."

"I thought all the Jews were poor as church mice, I mean, synagogue mice. And I was told that the Ukrainians hated them."

The guide shook her head no. "Before the Second World War," she explained, "Zhoukva was a center of commerce, art, and religion, with Ukrainians, Poles and Jews—who numbered more than 4,500 and made up almost half of the population. But . . . you know what happened."

"No, I don't."

She took a deep breath. "After the Nazis came, few survived the Holocaust."

My mind went black. That's what always happens when I hear about the Holocaust. It was so monumental, so horrible, that I just perceive blackness. I had seen so many photos of the emaciated people who survived concentration camps, and the piles of corpses who didn't survive. Maybe my mind was protecting me from feeling. Intellectually, I understood. But emotionally, it was dark, abstract, and unreal.

"It is a very sad part of our history," the guide said.

I nodded. I took a deep breath. After a respectful silence, the guide continued her narrative.

"There's something else I think you'll want to know," she said. "The Polish King, John Sobieski, built the synagogue between 1692 and 1700. Surprising, yes? There are two stories that can explain why. First is that wealthy local Jews loaned him money for the war between Poland and Turkey. When it was over, he returned the money and also paid for the construction of the synagogue. The second version--and perhaps both are true--is that the king was very ill and a Jewish doctor healed him. To thank the savior of his health, he built the synagogue. So you see how important their presence was."

"Can we go there now?" I inquired.

"Yes, but first I must get the key from Olga Kuzmenko. Please wait for me."

I took a deep breath. Everyone had told me I would find nothing of interest, that the world of the *shtetl*s was long gone in Ukraine. And yet, by the second day, I was following a trail that led to a woman with a milk bottle who looked like a character in *Fiddler on the Roof*, a Chernobyl survivor who hugged me as though she knew me, and a town where Jews had enough money to finance a war and ingratiate themselves with the king.

When our guide re-appeared, triumphantly holding the key, we followed her to a rare example of Renaissance Jewish architecture that once was one of the largest fortified synagogues in the world. The decaying outer walls were pale, delicate pink with off-white trim and sculptural elements. The inner walls were crowned with cupolas and arches. In 1941, the Nazis bombed the inside of the synagogue, and after that it languished on a list of endangered sites. There was evidence of scaffolding and restoration.

We walked gingerly inside the sanctuary with its graceful, vaulted ceiling, and saw the remains of the ark, which was surrounded by ornamental flowers. The Torah that was lovingly encased in the ark was long gone. In the center of the sanctuary were four brick columns, and within the columns there was once a *bimah*, a raised area, where the Torah was read. On the Eastern wall was a painting of Jerusalem and texts from prayers.

"The synagogue was built two meters (six feet) into the ground," our guide said, "because it was against the law to construct a house of worship higher than the churches."

Maybe the tri-cultural story wasn't so rosy, I thought. Perhaps the Jews were always on shaky terrain. And then they ended up six feet underground, like their synagogue.

In Orthodox synagogues, the men sit downstairs and I wanted to see where the women prayed, so we walked up an unstable flight of stairs to the women's section, where the floor felt as though it could collapse at any moment. The women sat behind a metal screen so they were separated from and not a distraction for the men who prayed on the main floor. A hole led from the women's balcony to the floor of the synagogue below; our guide said they often dropped gifts or money through the hole, destined for a boy on the occasion of his *Bar Mitzvah*.

"This is the first time I have ever been in a synagogue," Andrew said. "Everything is new to me and quite interesting. It's like a blessing. There are many more things I would like to say about it, but I don't have the English. I'm like a dog who understands everything and can't speak."

I smiled and grabbed Andrew's arm. "Your English is wonderful, and so are you. It's a deep pleasure for me to have you learn with us about our ancestry and how Jews lived in Ukraine."

That night, at the Kupol restaurant in L'viv, over *dor blu* (thick soup with sorrel and Danish blue cheese), *golubtsi* (cabbage rolls stuffed with wild rice and mushrooms, and topped with a tomato-based sauce), tender, braised pork with applesauce and broccoli, and Apple Charlotte with custard sauce, Andrew explained to Oksana in Ukrainian what we did in Zhoukva, and how mesmerized we were by the countryside. After talking to each other animatedly, they decided to take us to the foothills of the Carpathian Mountains to visit friends of theirs the next day.

"Oksana will visit with our friends," Andrew explained, "and we can explore the area."

"Do you think there is . . . I mean, is it a historic region ... is the culture intact?"

Andrew grinned and said, "Don't worry. I see how you are now that I have met you. I thought you were someone who traveled for work and wrote about nice hotels and restaurants. I believed you would have a superficial interest in Ukraine. Now I see that something drives you. I know that tomorrow you will find clues or something from the world of your grandmother."

"Thank you," I said. "Deeply, Andrew, thank you."

Andrew, Oksana and her marvelous *borscht.*

Unnerving souvenirs of a nesting doll of Hitler next to one of an Orthodox Jew.

Objects from the past used in daily life: *pais* (sidelock) curler and spectacles.

Meeting Alex, Vitaly (and the van) for the first time.

CHAPTER NINE -- URBAN ANCESTORS

I was taken aback when I first met Alex Denisenko. He drove up in front of Andrew and Oksana's house, and alit from the van that would transport us through Ukraine. Alex was a short, wiry, energetic man, dressed in sandals, beige shorts, and calf-high black socks.

"How can I have a guide who wears black socks?" I wondered silently. I am no fashion plate, *au contraire*, and I schlep around in sweatshirts, wearing fleece-lined Crocs in the winter, but even I have a bottom line. The last time I had a sartorial meltdown was almost three decades ago when I met Paul for the first time. He showed up wearing …plaid pants. I gulped. I tried to focus on what was above his belt, and we had the craziest, funniest date imaginable, but I couldn't get past those plaid pants. I told my friends that I had probably met my soul mate, but how could I spend my life with a man whose limbs were encased in plaid? Finally, I said it to Paul's face. We were at his apartment, and I couldn't hold it in any longer. I screwed up my courage and said, "I think you are terrific. You're funny and smart and highly creative. I like everything about you except the fact that you showed up for our first date in plaid."

"You didn't like those pants?" he said.

Uh-oh, I thought. I should have kept my big yap shut.

"So you didn't like those pants?" he repeated, and exited the room. He came back two minutes later with the plaid pants over his arm.

What's next? I wondered.

What came next was that Paul shredded the pants in front of me with his bare hands. His plaid pants lay in a heap of small pieces at his feet. We both howled with laughter. And we got married.

So although Alex's black socks were an eyesore, his English was excellent and his knowledge was encyclopedic. He would have been the perfect guide, except that the content of what he said was highly academic, rapid-fire and professorial as though he were making a report to a committee, or teaching a graduate class.

"Oh, no," I thought. "I'm making a pilgrimage of the heart, and our guide is taking us on a voyage of the head."

His credentials as a researcher were impeccable; he spent long hours in archives researching ancestry for clients, compromising his eyesight. He had the right lineage: His mother was a Russian Jew, so that opened doors and gave him access into the world of the *shtetls* that intrigued me. But how would my heart connect to his head? I wanted to feel; he wanted to inform.

The arrangement we had was that we would visit L'viv for one day with Alex and our driver Vitaly. Then we would spend a day with Andrew and Oksana, the only time their friends could receive us in the countryside. The following morning, bright and early, Alex would pick us up at Andrew's house and we would begin our voyage through the body of western Ukraine and into the heart of Minkowitz.

We climbed into the car, shook hands with handsome, easy-going Vitaly, and embarked on a whirlwind tour of L'viv. Information poured out of Alex, and I struggled to write it all down before the next wave of data, dates and discourse rolled in. I shot a panicked glance at Paul. I didn't have to explain. He just knew.

"Let's wait and see what happens," he whispered.

Alex said that some of the streets in L'viv are paved with stones made from the headstones of Jewish cemeteries, which were set in place by forced laborers under the Nazis. He led us to Tsurim Gilot, which is an active synagogue, and the only one that was in fairly good condition at the end of World War II; before the Nazi occupation there had been 47 synagogues. In 1938, there were 138,000 Jews in the city, and they made up 30 percent of the population. By 1944, after most of them had been murdered or deported, only 6,000 were left. Today there are about 3,000 Jews, and most of them come from Eastern Ukraine, Russia and Moldova.

"There was a higher death rate in L'viv than in any other city occupied by the Germans," Alex said.

Oh, God, I thought. The Jewish population of the city was almost entirely wiped out. The number of dead is twice the population of Santa Fe, the city where I live. So much loss and pain. So much suffering and misery and Holocaust horror. I knew it, I acknowledged it. I repeated it. But I couldn't feel it. Whenever I confronted the Holocaust, I felt guilty because I just went numb. It was too enormous. I knew what I was supposed to feel, but inside, there was only the void.

I thought about a young Canadian man I had met at Auschwitz in Poland. He carried a fiddle under his arm, and told me his grandmother had perished in the Holocaust but it wasn't real for him. He wanted to feel it, to internalize what her extermination meant. He said he hoped that through his music he could access his emotions. I bore witness as he stood between two rows of barbed wire, his eyes closed, playing a Yiddish melody, trying to evoke his grandmother's memory and what she had endured. When I left, he was still playing. I wonder if he succeeded.

I recalled the awful experience I had when I visited Dachau, the first concentration camp opened in Germany, when I was in my early twenties. I had never had any direct experience with anti-Semitism, and I was frustrated that my parents wouldn't let me get a German typewriter when I was in my early teens. World War II and the Nazis existed on another planet from the one I inhabited.

The night before I visited the camp at Dachau, I was in a bar in Munich, and two German men sat down at my table. They asked if I came from America, and I said yes. They leaned in close and asked me if I knew any Jews. I sort of shrugged, not sure what to answer. One of the men rubbed his two index fingers together. "Jews are like this," he said. "They always stick together. They control everything." "Hitler should have finished the job and killed all of them," said the second.

I was stunned, mortified. I couldn't believe what I was hearing. That night, I barricaded the door of my Munich hotel room with a chair, a lamp and a small wooden desk. I was terrified someone would come in to get me.

The next day, I visited Dachau in bone-chilling weather. I

walked in a daze through the barracks where inmates had been crammed in like animals. I tried to imagine Jews, Catholic priests, political prisoners, in thin clothes and sometimes without socks or shoes, starving, sick, desperate, freezing and keeling over in the snow. When I got to the crematoria, I was shocked to see that they looked like pizza ovens, but instead of pizzas, bodies were shoved in and incinerated, to hide the evidence of their death. I could almost hear the firing of the executioners' guns. I started to shake, and then I got numb. I couldn't feel anything. I was too young and it was too horrible. It was a long time before I could relate the experience to German friends I had later in life. One of them wept, and the other retreated into stone silence.

"The first Jews in the area appeared in the middle of the fourteenth century," Alex said. My fingers were starting to cramp up from writing everything Alex said in my tiny notebook. I felt as though every syllable mattered, that every word was a piece of the puzzle of the world my grandmother came from. "They were fleeing from Germany at the time of the Black Plague because they had been accused of poisoning the wells and bringing on the Plague."

The idea of people sneaking around, poisoning wells, deliberately spreading the Plague would be ludicrous if it weren't so disastrous for the accused. Why were Jews always blamed, judged and murdered for heinous, preposterous crimes like baking the blood of children into Passover *matzas*, spreading disease, poisoning wells?

At the Museum of Jewish Heritage, we were greeted by Olga, an educator and history buff, who told us how excited she was to have her job at the museum. Except for one survivor, her grandmother's family was wiped out by the Nazis. Her parents were completely assimilated and she learned little about her religion and culture. But now she is learning, and passing on the information to her children, she reported. She tries to teach them about traditions and holidays and dietary laws. "They are so receptive. They absorb everything and have become a hundred percent Jewish. When I bring food home to them, they say, 'Mommy, it's not kosher.' Sometimes things skip a generation."

What Olga told us next flew in the face of every stereotype I had in my mind about Eastern European Jews during the lifetime of my grandmother, and it reinforced what I had heard in Zhoukva. A world removed from the grinding poverty and ramshackle houses of *shtetl* inhabitants, the Jews of L'viv were very involved in the *Haskalah*, or Jewish Enlightenment, which combined Jewish traditions with Western culture. There were exuberant expansions in education, science, building, politics, the arts. Jews owned factories, movie houses, and construction companies. One of them started a vodka factory that is still functioning. There were two Yiddish theatres, where women acted alongside of men, classical dramas, like Shakespeare's plays, and Russian works like those by Chekhov, Tolstoy, and other playwrights. Sholem Aleichem (whose stories about Tevye the Milkman formed the basis of *Fiddler on the Roof*), lived in L'viv for six months before moving to America; his plays were rejected because he wasn't a good enough businessman to promote them. Some Jews were Orthodox and others were Reform or assimilated, like Olga's family.

"You mean...they were urban people? Upwardly mobile, literati and artists and businessmen, integrated into the fabric of L'viv?" I asked with incredulity. As I write this, it seems obvious, but I had no idea that Jewish people were not all living the Minkowitz lifestyle. I thought they were all like my grandmother. No one had ever mentioned to me that there were rich, highly educated, successful Jews.

Olga nodded, and then showed us objects that were used in daily life: a sewing machine, bookshelves, an iron with a Jewish star hidden inside, a Yiddish typewriter that moved from right to left, scissors for cutting candles, *pais* curlers that were used to create curls in the Orthodox men's sidelocks. There were fragments from *Torah*s that were left behind when Jews were sent to concentration camps. Some of them were given to Gentile Ukrainian neighbors, who preserved them at great peril. They didn't even tell their children they had them, because it would have been too dangerous to divulge under Nazi and Russian occupation. The children grew up and found the fragments when they were decorating their home about ten years ago. Now they were preserved in the museum, part of the history of the Jewish people.

I was mesmerized by the objects. They were real, tangible, not just ideas. When I touched them, it was like Proust eating the Madeleine cookie; they transported me back to Minkowitz. I pictured fathers curling their sons' sidelocks, mothers cutting candles. There were not enough objects in the world to satisfy my craving to know and feel what life was like for my grandmother and her family.

Olga showed us photos that told the story of what happened to the Jews in L'viv. The Nazis made a short film that screened in movie theatres. It showed a rich woman wearing a fur coat; when the camera zoomed in, it revealed fleas in the fur. The message was that Jews, even rich ones, were filthy and brought fleas. The Soviets, too, were no slouches at whipping up anti-Semitism. They executed Ukrainians and Poles and lied about it, blaming Jews for the murders.

Olga explained that L'viv had the distinction of being a city that had a ghetto, concentration, and extermination camps. It was unusual to have that troika of oppressive misery in one place. The Nazis hanged the leader of the *Judenrat* (council) and then photographed his limp, inert body. Several hundred Jews survived by living in the filth of the sewers. It was so terrible, so hard to take in, so impossible to imagine, I closed my eyes and took a deep breath, praying Olga would say something heartening. She must have sensed my dismay, because seconds later she reported some positive, life-affirming information. 2,400 certificates were issued to Ukrainians for being among the righteous of the nations; this was an honor bestowed by the state of Israel on Gentile people who risked their lives to save Jews from being exterminated by the Nazis.

"We're going to the outskirts of L'viv," Alex informed us. Vitaly drove us to the site of the Janowska concentration camp, and Alex filled us in on the gruesome details.

"When Jews were transported here on street cars, they were separated into categories of necessary and unnecessary. Writers and rabbis and intellectuals were killed first, because they were disposable. People with technical and engineering skills or those who could do hard work were more important and could be used. Simon Wiesenthal — the concentration camp survivor who documented the atrocities of the Nazis and dedicated his life to tracking down the ones who were alive and had not been brought to justice — was a laborer here. He helped to build the buildings," Alex explained.

It was not lost on me or Paul that we would have been killed first. So, for that matter, would Alex. And most of my friends. And family. And all my teachers. And authors whose books I loved. And many of the people I admired.

Alex pointed to a hill and the place where there was a long trench. The Jewish prisoners stood on top of the hill, were shot, and fell into the trench. "They even made Jewish musicians play music as they were shot. It was called the 'Tango of Death.' They also ran truck engines and machine engines so the shooting couldn't be heard outside the camp. About 90,000 people were killed here. In 1943, after the defeat of the Germans in the battle of Stalingrad, the Nazis had the Jews dig up the bodies, burn them, and grind them to destroy the evidence. Simon Wiesenthal worked at this horrible job. On the spot where we are standing, Nazis threw pieces of bread to starving Jews to taunt them. When they rushed at the bread, they were shot," Alex said.

How can a human mind wrap around this? I registered the horror and the cruelty, but I couldn't feel. I couldn't feel anything. Why wasn't it real to me? What was wrong with me? I am Jewish. Six million Jews were slaughtered. I was listening to Alex describe some of the events in lurid detail, but it remained abstract, elusive, a gigantic ball of atrocity and pain that bounced right through me and then bounced away

I had tried to feel the reality of the Holocaust since I was a young child. I remember staring at photos of piles of human cadavers, my eyes widening at the skeletal remains, which were little more than bones covered by a thin layer of flesh. When I took a shower, I turned up the hot water until it was scalding, and I tried to stand in the water stream as long as I could to prepare myself for the eventuality that I would be sent to an extermination camp. In my mind, the showers infused with lethal Zyklon B gas were scalding, and I wanted to prepare to survive them. I didn't understand that there was never any water in the showers, and that the inmates were told they were going to a shower, but they were heading to a deadly rendezvous with Zyklon B gas. How do African-Americans, Armenians, Rwandans, Irish — all the populations decimated by torture, murder and annihilation — deal with the pain of their peoples' past?

I was grateful when we stopped for lunch, because I needed a break from Holocaust horrors and from lacerating myself because I couldn't respond.

"Alex," I said, "I don't want the Nazi atrocities to be the focus of this trip."

He nodded. I hoped he understood. I marveled at his stamina. As soon as the meal was over, he continued the tour, cramming in as much as possible.

"I think this will interest you," Alex postulated as we entered a synagogue that was built in the early nineteenth century. The ceilings were about 50 feet high; light streamed in through huge windows. A young man named Alex Nazar greeted us, and told us that the synagogue had been turned into a horse stable by the Nazis. He explained that after the Second World War, there was a huge influx of Jews from Russia and Eastern Ukraine. They arrived in large cities to find work in Soviet industries. Also, because so many Jews had been murdered, there were many flats available. People called the apartments and land of the exterminated Jews 'blood lands.' People didn't ask who had lived there before," he said. "The less you knew, the better."

Alex Nazar said he was the head of a group of young people with Jewish family lineage who were restoring the synagogue, doing the physical labor themselves. They get no official support. Part of their fundraising involved joyous celebrations. In fact, they had just finished four days of "*Yiddishkeit*" festivities with Yiddish films and klezmer music, where words of songs were projected onto the walls so everyone could read them and sing along. Other non-Jewish institutions joined in the event, which was very heartening to hear.

"We are not sure what we will do with the building once it is restored," Alex said. "Maybe it will become a social center."

Yes, I thought, yes, yes, yes. Young people are moving forward, turning tragedy into joy. Not just looking back at the nightmare of the past, but physically constructing a dream for the future. I recalled a very cool, trendy, smart, young Jewish man I had met in Budapest. He worked in fashion, television and publishing.

"I'm not focused on the Holocaust," he said. "My grandmother perished at the hands of the Nazis, and I feel sad and horrible about that. I will never ever forget. But how can you get young people interested in Jewish culture if all you do is dwell on the horror of the past? I am looking ahead, to the future. I want it to be joyous and fun, not tragic. That's where my friends and I are focused."

We followed Alex through the area of L'viv where the Jews used to live; past the section where the ritual slaughterers used to be, past the street which used to house the *mikvahs*, or ritual baths, and the street that was once home to several different synagogues. We had to use our imaginations to conjure up the ghosts that howled and wept underneath what is now a modern city. We had to visualize that the central market was on the spot where the Jewish cemetery used to be, and where Jewish bones still lie. We came to the house where Sholem Aleichem had dwelled and written two plays (unproduced in L'viv, as we learned from Olga). A plaque on the wall commemorating him included images of the *shtetl* characters he wrote about. They were itinerant, moving from one place to another.

"Wait, Alex," I called to him as he walked on. "I want to spend a little more time here."

What was it about anything having to do with *shtetl* life that grabbed my soul? Even inert images incised on a plaque. Of course I needed to know about what happened to the Jews who remained behind, and who suffered and perished during the Nazi and Soviet occupations. I wanted to have deeper knowledge about the whole area, and report back with first-hand information to people who never had the fortune I did, to actually walk the land, learning, absorbing, seeing, visiting, interviewing, recording. About the *shtetl*s, I could feel. About the Holocaust, I became a horrified shell with no emotion.

I thought back to a Czech man named Alex—Why was everyone suddenly named Alex?—who lived with my family for about six months when I was a teenager. My parents took him in and never charged him a dime. They felt sorry for him because he was a concentration camp survivor. He was brusque, cold, and fairly unpleasant. One day, Alex was heading outside, and it was raining. My mother handed him an umbrella, and he brushed it away. "What do I need an umbrella for?" he snapped. "When I was a child in the camp, a Nazi guard came up to me one day and handed me a box of matches. 'Those are the ashes of your father,' he told me, laughing cruelly, as I stared at the ashes. After that, who cares about an umbrella?" And he walked out the door, as my mother sighed heavily. I understood that he was broken inside, and it explained his coldness and dour demeanor.

I remembered a story a man told me about ten years ago. He said his father had been one of the American soldiers who liberated an extermination camp. His father never spoke about it. One day, fifty years after the liberation, the father told his son, "We dug a hole and buried the bodies. Those of us who dug never said a word. We never looked at each other. We were so ashamed of being human."

"I have something unusual to show you," Alex said, interrupting my bleak reveries. We walked to the Lazarus Rappoport Hospital, a vast building constructed between 1906 and 1908 in the Historicist mode, which was vibrant and eclectic, inspired by different architectural styles from the past. Most striking about the hospital was the dome and the Moorish style, which was an architectural nod to the Jews who came from North Africa. Jewish stars surrounded the cupola. Lazarus and Rappoport were wealthy, secular Jews who wanted to show solidarity with their culture and the Jewish community.

Alex was right. It was unusual. On the ground on one side of the hospital was an accumulation of pieces of cemetery headstones that had just been found. Apparently, a man had purchased stones to use as construction material for his new house. His neighbor recognized that he was using pieces of tombstones that had once been in the Jewish cemetery, which dated back to 1414. The man had a conscience and donated the stones. They lie in the earth now, until it is decided what to do with them. Several ideas are floating around, one of which is building a wall of tribute to Jews.

"There is now much more awareness of the destruction of Jewish material culture. There is an attempt to restore cemeteries and preserve Jewish history. This is happening in a few places in western Ukraine, and it is influenced by the preservation efforts in Poland," Alex noted. "But unfortunately, there are beautiful Jewish buildings here that are falling into disrepair and nothing is being done about them. A wonderful exception is the Golden Rose Synagogue, which is now a protected UNESCO World Heritage site. They were going to build a hotel on the site, but world outcry made them stop the construction, and it is now preserved. We will go there together before we leave L'viv for our trip through Ukraine."

Architecture. Headstones. Material culture. Poland. Preservation. My brain was swirling. We went to the Golden Rose

Synagogue. We also passed by old buildings that once housed a Jewish theatre, and the milk hall, where milk products were sold in the 1800's. The signs on the outside in Yiddish, Polish, and German were still visible.

The sun went down, and Alex said Vitaly would take us back to Andrew's house.

"Thank you for a very complex and informative day," I said to Alex.

He nodded modestly.

When we got back to Andrew's house, I collapsed on the bed, near tears. Andrew asked me what was wrong, and it all came pouring out. How this trip had been a dream since childhood. How I wanted to connect so badly to the life of the *shtetl*s and the world of my grandmother. How Alex was brimming with information, a brilliant guide and scholar. But how this trip was all about my heart, not just information. Alex was feeding my head. I wanted to feed my heart.

Andrew smiled gently.

"Judith," he said, "this is just the first day. Maybe Alex is intellectual and he is in his head. But I have a feeling that after spending time with you two, he will change, and he will be a man of the heart."

I choked back my tears.

"Andrew, you are the best pen pal any woman ever had."

Like Alex, he smiled modestly.

Barbara Paraska's life is similar to that of the ancestors

CHAPTER TEN -- SOUL FOOD

The following day, Oksana packed a cooler full of snacks—for her, food accompanies all human activities— and we drove south towards the Carpathian Mountains in the direction of the Hungarian border. As we rode along, we noticed that almost every house had a large vegetable garden and conical haystacks to feed the cows that produced milk and beef.

"Nice, fresh food is very important to the Ukrainian," Andrew commented.

We arrived at the sprawling, designer country house of Igor and Hala. The former combined his expertise in architecture and engineering to build his dream house of stone, wood and cement.

After everyone hugged us hello, their daughter and son-in-law invited us on a walk into the fields. At first we spoke a bit about the son-in-law's work as an abdominal surgeon. His salary is a paltry $200 a month, but patients know this and give the surgeons tips or "bribes." The daughter showed us their favorite spots for gathering mushrooms that they use to make mushroom soup and sauces.

"Good, fresh food is very important to Ukrainians," the duo explained, echoing the words Andrew had used a few hours before.

We returned to the house and gathered around a large wooden

table on the outdoor deck. Before eating, we each had a few shooters of vodka—with instructions to finish the whole glass at once, rather than sipping it— followed by *borscht* that was served with raw garlic cloves. I got the vodka down in two gulps, rather than one, and figured we'd all stink so I threw self-consciousness to the wind and ate about five cloves of garlic.

As soon as I finished swallowing, Hala appeared with a plate of kasha pastries.

"This is like the kasha knishes I ate as a kid!" I exclaimed.

On its heels came wild rice, chicken croquets, meat croquets and a discussion about the reason we had come to their country— my preoccupation with my grandmother and her *shtetl*— and the similarities between the Jewish food I was raised with, and some favorite Ukrainian comestibles. The more vodka I drank, the more voluble I became.

I began by telling them about my grandmother's kitchen in Brooklyn, with its buckling linoleum floor and fluorescent light fixture. When I visited her, I used to stick my nose into the pot to watch the throat, stomach, feet, and little golden eggs of the chicken swirling around in the boiling water that would become chicken soup.

Another specialty was roast chicken, and, as with all her cooking, it was spiced almost imperceptibly with salt, pepper, and garlic. She only cooked with chickens that came from a kosher butcher, and she first had to soak them in salt and drain the blood. Then she removed the thick, yellow globs of fat, and rendered them in a pan with onions. The fat would melt and mix with the onions, and she poured the concoction into a glass jar and put it in the refrigerator. When it became solid, it was used as a spread—instead of butter—on bread, and it was called *schmaltz*.

"*Shmaltz!*" exclaimed Andrew. "We love *schmaltz*. We make it from pig fat!"

"Pig fat?? My grandmother—wherever she is— is covering her ears right now so she doesn't hear the name of the forbidden food!" I exclaimed.

"At Passover time," I continued, "my grandmother prepared gefilte fish—a poached, oval fish ball that was made from de-boned, ground pike, whitefish, and carp. It was served with "*chrain*," or horseradish."

"Yes, *chrain*, that's what we call it too!" announced Andrew.

I explained that my grandmother also made *matza* meal bagels, and I loved to stand and watch her drop them into boiling water to cook.

For Chanukah, she fried potatoes to make patties called *latkas*.

"*Platzkes!*" Igor bellowed, and we all roared.

On Friday, for the Sabbath, my grandmother sometimes made *kugel*, which was a sort of egg noodle pudding that baked in the oven until the outside of the noodles became crisp. It was a very dense dish and, when served piping hot with *kishka*, which is made by stuffing animal intestines with flour, spices, leftovers, and God knows what else, the effect on the body is like consuming tasty molten lead.

"*Kishke*," Hala repeated, and she ran off the kitchen to bring us some to taste. It was made from stuffed intestines and had blood inside of it, which made me wince a bit, but I nibbled at it politely.

Somehow, the food similarities reassured me that I was, indeed, in the land my ancestors came from, and that the *shtetl* folks ate the food of the people around them. I wondered who influenced whom, and if any of the dishes originated in the *shtetl*s and became widespread— like bagels or *blintzes* in America today—or if the Jews just adapted their neighbors' foods.

"Do you still use family recipes in your cooking?" I asked Hala.

"The *borscht* we ate today came straight from my grandmother."

I said that in my family, the recipes were handed down from mother to daughter, from my great-great-grandmother to my great-grandmother, from my great-grandmother to my grandmother, from my grandmother to my mother, which meant that at home, growing up, I ate ancestral recipes, prepared and embellished by my mother. The kitchen of my house was the site where my mother patiently drained the blood from chickens, chopped meat in a wooden bowl, and made liver and onions, stuffed veal, meatballs and spaghetti, filet of flounder, and baked apples.

When we had finished our meal and our delightful comparison of edibles, Igor and Hala's family went inside, and Paul and I opted to remain outside on the deck, looking out over the land. The lunchtime conversation about food triggered childhood memories of abuse and punishment in the kitchen. I didn't like to think about them, and I rarely discussed them with others. I was surprised that they came, unbidden, from the past.

I recalled that I almost always ate ravenously; I suppose I was in need of emotional nourishment that I couldn't get through normal channels. I remembered one time when my mother cancelled my tenth birthday party and forced me to call all my friends and tell them what an awful child I was. I refused to do it, determined not to let my mother get the better of me. Instead of crying and screaming, I devised a plan to make the party without my mother. I took every penny I owned—I think it amounted to about 6 dollars, walked to the Five & Dime store, and bought little bags full of Good & Plenty licorice candies in different colors. Then I proceeded to the butcher, and purchased as many frankfurters (hotdogs) as I could afford with the remaining money. I came home, went directly to the kitchen, cut the hotdogs up into half-inch slices, put a pot on the stove to boil them, poured the Good & Plenty candies into bowls, and prepared for my guests.

My mother came into the kitchen, saw what I was doing, dragged me outside, through the backyard, and locked me in the garage. It was dark and menacing in the garage; the upright rakes and lawnmower and hoses looked ominous. I was terrified. I think my hope for maternal love died that night, and a part of me rose out of the garage, floated over the rooftop, and disappeared for decades. It went to a realm where I was safe, where my mother's eyes didn't grow cold as she punished or beat me. What replaced the part of me that went away was fear and anxiety, which resulted from a profound feeling of aloneness and lack of safety. I never knew what would come at me next.

Two days after my traumatic tenth birthday, things were back to normal in my house, or what I thought was normal at the time, because I hadn't been raised in any other house and couldn't compare. I sat in the kitchen while my mother was cooking and telling compelling, entertaining stories. I devoured raw, freshly-chopped meat and uncooked *kugel*. I stuffed my young face, trying to get from my mother's food what I couldn't get from her.

I never told anyone about what was going on inside my home. And I am sure I never told my grandmother, but she knew what a formidable adversary my mother was. "When she was three years old," she told me once again, "she decided to raise herself. And she did. Nobody ever told your mother what to do."

Why hadn't I told my grandmother? Why did I feel obliged to keep the truth a secret?

My father died when I was 20, and then there was no one standing between me and my mother. It was very uncomfortable for me to sit on the deck, reliving the pain of growing up in my house. I didn't ordinarily think about it, but somehow, being in the land of my forebears made me access aspects of self that I thought were healed and no longer had an impact on my life. I was dismayed that they were still so close to the surface. I wondered if childhood could ever be healed, or if it continued forever to ooze and seep into adult life?

I was relieved when Igor and Hala's daughter and son-in-law came outside and said they knew I was interested in history and authenticity in Ukraine and offered to take us to visit a very elderly woman who lived nearby. I eagerly agreed.

We walked down a dirt road to the dilapidated wooden home of Barbara Paraska, a very poor and welcoming woman, who at age 90, was frail, bent over, walked with a cane, and yet, remarkably, lived alone. She said that last year she sold her cow, and before that she had to sell her horses. Now she only had two goats and a few chickens left.

We asked Barbara about her life and she willingly told us that at age 20 she was exiled to Siberia for eight years to build roads. She was being punished for the crime of bringing food to Ukrainian soldiers who were in the forest, fighting communism. "Under Stalin, we were treated terribly," she said. "If our families didn't send us clothes, we would not have survived the winter."

I could not take my eyes off her, her house, and the crumbling wattle and daub barn adjacent to her house. I felt like crying when she spoke about her life and when I saw the penury she lived in.

"Minkowitz?" Paul whispered to me.

I nodded yes. "I'll bet this is what my grandmother's house was like," I whispered back excitedly.

"Barbara, were you born in this house?"

"Yes, and my parents lived in it before I was born."

I calculated that the house was at least a hundred years old, which meant that it was, yes, contemporaneous with the house where my grandmother lived. I held my hand over my heart; just standing there, with Barbara, outside her house, was deeply moving to me. I wondered if I would ever in my life be closer to the reality of what life was like in Minkowitz.

Barbara explained that she had family on the other side of the river who brought her food, which she accepted, but she would not leave her house to go and live with them.

We gently asked if we could see the inside of her house, and she agreed. As soon as I crossed the threshold, I felt overcome with sadness. The house was filthy. The kitchen was also used as a bedroom. The wooden floors were in a state of disrepair. A small wood-burning stove heated the house. Wood was piled in a storage space and covered with several yards of frayed, burgundy-colored material. Pots and pans were piled up everywhere, and the only place to sit was a wooden bench that was next to a long, wooden table. An armoire was the only other furniture in the room.

My mouth fell open when I saw what was on Barbara's bed: two overstuffed goose down comforters that were at least three or four feet high. My mother had told me that when my grandmother came from Minkowitz to the United States, one of her only possessions was a huge goose down comforter. I felt as though I were staring at it.

"Paul ..." I said. And I didn't have to finish the sentence. He looked at the comforters and he just knew.

I walked across a dirt floor to an adjacent room where I saw an open trunk that was overflowing with old clothes. On the wall was a Ukrainian carpet, religious art, and photos of Shevchenko and Franco, two famous Ukrainian poets. When she saw me looking at them, Barbara explained, "I fought all my life for Ukrainian independence."

When we walked outside again, we could see that Barbara was tired. I held her hands, looked into her eyes, and told her that this was a very important visit for me. I wished her health, and hugged her.

I didn't speak as we walked back to Igor and Hala's house. Andrew pierced the silence with a single comment. "I have been here to visit Igor and Hala many times," he said. "But I have never met Barbara, and I had no idea she lived nearby. I think you have a kind of magnet for the way Minkowitz once was. Everywhere we go, it finds you and attaches itself."

"Are you sure there is none of this left in Minkowitz?" I asked Andrew hopefully.

"No, it is gone."

As we walked, I vowed that somehow I would find it. Then I reflected that, in a sense, I was already finding it. The truth of my grandmother's life seemed to be emerging out of the Ukrainian landscape. And the truth of my life seemed to be emerging out of my inner landscape. I chose to make this trip, but I never imagined it would have such reverberating intensity.

Dunca, the last Jew standing

CHAPTER ELEVEN -- DUNCA: THE LAST JEW STANDING

Riding in the van with Alex was like having a reference library in the front seat. I kept looking at Alex's head, wondering how such a small skull could contain so much information, and how he could access it with such speed.

As we drove through the countryside of western Ukraine, Alex spoke to us about the Pale of Settlement. I had heard about it all my life—the region of Imperial Russia where Jews were permitted to live, and outside of which they were forbidden to settle—but it seemed remote, long ago, something you read about in history texts. Now I was actually in the area that used to comprise the Pale, and my imagination was on fire. It was present, immediate, palpable, right outside our car window. I understood the direct link between banishment from certain agricultural areas and large cities and the rise of the *shtetl* culture in Eastern Europe. I pictured Jews in rickety carts and wagons or on foot, carrying their meager possessions to small villages where they were permitted to exist. The Pale was a vast area that included present-day Poland, Belarus, Lithuania, Moldova, Ukraine, and parts of western Russia. At one point, before World War II, it contained five million inhabitants. My grandmother was one of them.

Catherine the Great created the Pale in the late eighteenth century. According to Alex, she was less of an anti-Semite than some of her predecessors, who tried to have all Jews banished from Russia unless they converted to Russian Orthodoxy. Alex confirmed what I had always heard— that the Czars despised and persecuted the Jews. He said that two of the Czars—Alexander I and Alexander II—were the best of the worst, a dubious distinction.

Although I'm pretty certain that most people in the Pale wanted to stay under the official radar, they had to participate in the very comprehensive censuses of 1835 and 1892, when all members of each family were listed. That probably made Herr Hitler's work much easier, as there were formal records to help rout out the undesirables.

Like most oppressed minorities, many Jews were very resourceful and enterprising. Some were well-paid tailors who stitched uniforms for the Czar's army. Others were university graduates, artisans, doctors, shoemakers, craftsmen or registered prostitutes; their professions were in such high demand that they were sometimes allowed to live in big cities and outside of the Pale. Some women actually lied and registered as prostitutes, although they weren't, so they could expand their horizons beyond the restricted Pale.

The one thing no one wanted was to be conscripted into the Czar's army. It was a 25-year stint; you went in as a young man and came out in middle age. Conditions and treatment were awful, and both Jews and Gentiles went to great extremes to avoid the hated service. Some purposely injured themselves or claimed to be insane. Others served in military intelligence or were spies; the latter helped Russia win the war against Napoleon. Many, like my paternal grandfather, were in the army and fled. It was one of the only things I knew about him: he had escaped the dreaded military service and somehow made his way to the United States.

It sounds colorful in retrospect to say that one's grandfather or great grandfather fled the Czar's army, but, in truth, I imagine that it involved great fear and sadness as young sons left their mamas, papas, and siblings, never knowing if they would meet again. The young men doubtless experienced deprivation, cold, hunger, loneliness, and anxiety before they reached a destination where they felt safe from the long arm of the Czar. For the first time, I felt sadness that I didn't learn more about my father's father. It was mostly because he spoke Yiddish. I wondered where he lived in the Pale of Settlement and what his life was like.

"I think it's time to tell you about two women from Rohatyn, the small city we are entering now," Alex said, interrupting my ruminations. I looked out the window and saw a sign with the name of the town.

"The first is Roxalana, and she is Rohatyn's most famous daughter. In the 1520's, Roxalana was captured by the Crimean Tatars and sold to Sultan Suleiman the Magnificent. She was at first a concubine in his harem, and eventually became his wife; her trajectory was the success story of a small town girl who evolved into one of the most powerful women in the history of the Ottoman

Empire. Today she is remembered in Rohatyn by a prominent statue.

"The second woman is the complete opposite of Roxalana," Alex explained. "She is the last remaining Jew and there is no glory in her life. It will be a very difficult visit. Are you sure it's agreeable to you?"

Paul and I nodded yes.

We walked to a gray stucco house with a brown mansard roof. The yard in front of it was partially covered with sparse grass. Straining on a heavy chain, and approaching too close to us for my comfort, was a snapping, barking dog. Picturing his teeth sinking into my shins, I refused to go any farther.

Alex called out to the woman of the house, but there was no answer. He took a few steps forward, and the dog leapt toward him. Alex jumped back.

Just as we were about to leave, an elderly woman with white hair, blue eyes, dressed in a purple, checkered, flannel shirt, a red sleeveless sweater and a green, checkered skirt, emerged from the house. Although she seemed frail and walked slowly, the moment she commanded the dog to quiet down, he ceased barking. She opened a brown gate and beckoned us to follow her inside. The dog kept his counsel, but followed us warily with his eyes.

The main room of her house served as a bedroom, sitting room, and kitchen, with the latter area off to the side. The room was cluttered with old furniture with the exception of a flat-screen TV. The floor was a mixture of old carpeting and worn vinyl.

"I am Dunca Reis," the woman said, and then introduced us

to her 50-year-old son, who, afflicted with cerebral palsy, squirmed in a wheelchair. We greeted him and introduced ourselves, but he was unable to speak.

Our hostess sat on the end of her bed. She invited us to sit on a sofa, facing her. We explained why we had come to Ukraine, and said it was an honor to meet someone who had survived the fate of 99% of the Rohatyn Jews at the hands of the Nazis.

"Survived?" Dunca said, almost to herself. "I am weak and sick, and my son, too, is sick. Who will care for him when I die? What will become of him? I am old now. I am very disappointed in my life."

She sat still, and folded one hand over the other. I noticed how long and graceful her fingers were.

There was nothing we could say. As fellow humans, who came from far away to spend a small slice of time with Dunca, how could we possibly respond?

"I am so sorry," I muttered.

She nodded, and then took a deep breath. "Would you like to hear my story?"

"Yes, please."

I wrote as fast as I could, trying to keep eye contact with Dunca, listening to her words, waiting for Alex's translations, and guessing at the spelling of the names of tiny villages Dunca mentioned.

"During the Holocaust, my father was a clerk. His job was to give permission for logging. I used to travel around to different villages with him while he dealt with the lumbermen. Sometimes we would stop to gather strawberries in the forest. I have good memories of those times."

Dunca reached for a stack of photos and showed us one of her father, sitting on a chair outside, dressed in a suit. He looked tall, robust, and had thick, blond hair. She stood next to him, a young girl, her long, brown hair braided neatly. They looked normal and happy.

"One day, when I was 10 or 11 years old, they rounded up all the Jews in the town square. I stayed with my mother and didn't go. Nearby was a teacher who taught me in my first year of school. She told my mother I could stay with her overnight. That night, they killed all the Jews. You could see blood running in the streets. It was 1942 or 1943. People said my mother had been killed at a well. I went to look for her but couldn't find her. All the bodies had been moved to a mass grave near the new cemetery.

"Terrified, I walked to some of the villages and arrived in Rodan. I knew a man from there because I had met him with my father, but he had been killed too. I stayed in the attic of his house for a month. His wife gave me food and never told her children I was there. They were afraid to hide me any longer and I had to go. I went to the village of Lipuka. People were leaving a church service when I got there, and I sat and cried by the church. The deacon came and took me by the hand. He said I could stay overnight but no longer, as he was afraid to keep me. The next day, he took me to a field and told me to go away. A woman from another village remembered my father and me. She took me to Zalanufe village and told me about a family in a remote area who would adopt me as a daughter if I cared for their livestock. I was not trained as a cowherd and was not good at it. I was once beaten when I let our cow go into a neighbor's yard, but generally I was fine with this new woman. They called her Marika and there was a boy my own age. She adopted me and registered me as her child. I was raised Christian.

"After the collapse of the Soviet system, I got back my father's property from before the Holocaust, but it was very neglected. My daughter and her family and I fixed it up and, as you see, I live here now. My husband died a long time ago."

She showed us her wedding picture, and we sank into stunned silence. She was so young and lovely. Her long, flowing brown hair was crowned with a tiara of fresh flowers. Her husband looked young, confident, and handsome. It was such a painful contrast to the wretchedness of the present.

"You see that I have icons in my house, because I was raised Christian, but I consider myself Jewish. I come from Jewish parents who were killed for being Jewish. The Jews help me through their charities. I get food from the Joint Distribution Committee and assistance from Chesed. I depend on their help because I spend my whole pension on food. My daughter lives in the house next door and has a spinal cord injury. My main interest is to help my son. I am moving toward death. I am 78. I once had a heart attack. The ambulance came and got me. I have a shelf of medications I need to take, a whole pharmacy here. Last year I fell and hit my head and now I have headaches all the time."

Dunca stopped speaking. I realized how much energy it had taken her to relive awful memories and tell us her story. It was a bare bones narrative of a horrible series of events, but each of them was somehow infused with a small ray of hope and an enormous amount of courage. Why did she tell her story to strangers? Maybe she wanted witnesses to her life. Perhaps she wanted us to tell it to others, so her life would not be in vain, and she would not be forgotten. Perhaps I could help her in some small way.

"Dunca, is it okay if I write about what you are telling us? You are very important. You are the last link to the story of what happened here."

She closed her eyes and slowly nodded yes.

Alex was right. It was a very hard visit. Dunca seemed so much older than 78 years. She had suffered greatly in her life, and the suffering continued every day, relentlessly.

"Dunca, would you mind if we took a photo of you?"

"Wait a moment."

She reached behind her and picked up a burgundy babushka, which she draped around her head and tied beneath her chin. She wanted to look good for the photo. Her eyes sparkled as Paul recorded a moment in her existence. I loved seeing her little vanity, a sign of pride, and of life.

After we left Dunca's house, it was difficult to shake the heaviness of her situation and her story. I had met survivors before, but it was the first time I was ever in the presence of a survivor in the place where it happened, in the town, near the square where so many had been murdered. Sitting in her house, looking at photos of her loved ones who had been murdered, knowing she was the last remaining Jew in a town where thousands once flourished, was a terrifying experience.

"I feel the same way," Paul sighed. I hadn't said a word to him, but he had the same reaction.

The heaviness we felt in Dunca's house stayed with us and hung in the car as we rode away. It was an in-your-face confrontation with the Holocaust. I tried to push it away as I always did, and, once again, succumbed to feelings of numbness and distance. What was wrong with me? Even though I had sat in Dunca's house, listening to her terrible story of loss and survival, I couldn't connect emotionally to the ghastly reality of what she and others had experienced. It was too big to comprehend. Too removed from the reality I had known.

I wanted to focus on Minkowitz, and life in the *shtetl* before the Fiddler fell off the Roof. I could easily connect to that because it was colorful and, despite the poverty and insecurity, it was alive and vital, sprinkled with humor and earthy food. I wanted to push away everything that happened after my grandmother left her *shtetl*. But as we visited more sites, met more people, and heard more horror stories, it became increasingly difficult. I tried to focus on the facts I was hearing so I wouldn't be dragged down into an emotional abyss. Numbness was my friend, my protector.

Stopping to experience a bit of the service at the Holy Virgin Church for Corpus Christi day was a welcome distraction from my dismal thoughts. The local congregants carried large wreaths into the church, and the priest blessed them.

"It seems you enjoy watching how they celebrate a holiday in a Ukrainian church," Alex observed.

"I love witnessing and experiencing all kinds of religious and spiritual traditions," I said.

"Then you will probably want to visit the Karaite cemetery in Halych."

I did, indeed. In our travels, I had encountered Karaite practitioners, and, although I knew little about them, I was intrigued that they identified themselves as Karaite Jews. When I mentioned Karaites to a few rabbis I knew, their response was rather negative so I stopped mentioning them. When I hear that two groups are polarized and antagonistic, I tend to back away, get whatever objective information I can, and not get involved in the politics of opposition.

In my limited understanding, the Jewish Karaites adhere to what is written in the Torah and reject rabbinic oral law. Rabbinic Jews reject the Karaites. They both believe in a Messianic era, but the path to get there diverged in the eighth century.

"The Nazis didn't wipe out the Karaites because they mistakenly thought they were Turkic, and not Semitic," Alex reported.

We had to jump a wooden fence to enter the Karaite cemetery, located in a picturesque spot, overlooking the top of a castle and a pre-war bridge that spanned the Dnieper River. As I wandered among the stones, I realized that they looked like Jewish headstones, and were ornamented with familiar symbols like lions, birds, a crown, a tree, a candelabrum, a Jewish star. I read the names on the stones: Abrahamovich, Eszwowicz, Ickowicz, Charzenko, Kozulina. Some of them had dates as recent as 2009, and others, which were older, were used as supports to prop up haystacks.

The longer we lingered in the cemetery, the more I thought about the religious beliefs that separate people and how, carried to the extreme, they could result in the annihilation of one people by another. That was what happened to Dunca's family, to Dunca, and to the Jews of Rohatyn and L'viv. Why does anyone care if God is worshipped differently, or if others worship a different God? How do humans descend to such a dark place that they kill other humans because they sit in pews or kneel to pray, wear sidelocks, monks' robes or turbans, read from the Hebrew Bible, the New Testament, or the Koran? How can groups of people be so threatened and demented that they persecute other groups of people because their holidays, dietary laws, clothes, prophets, and teachings are unfamiliar? I was buffeted by waves of sadness that I couldn't stop. I was positively maudlin as I pondered the huge pie that is life, and why groups of humans aren't content with their slice.

When we got back into the car, there must have been a black cloud visible around me. We stopped at towns with a barely surviving synagogue where dozens used to stand before the war, and visited the paltry remnants of once-thriving Jewish neighborhoods. It was hard not to succumb to the lure of dark reflection about the underbelly of human nature, which is lined with hatred, intolerance, ignorance, entitlement, and violence. It also occurred to me that the people we met were links to the past of Eastern Europe, and they carried the precious stories of where we come from and who preceded us. They bore witness to once-vibrant people and communities that were annihilated. What they learned came from life and personal experience. When they were gone, the link would be broken. Who would remember the past? Who would tell the stories we were hearing of loss and survival? Who would remember odd facts told to little girls by their grandmothers who came long ago from *shtetls* like Minkowitz?

The urgency I felt about my trip returned, and I focused on the present more than ever, attentive to everything I saw, every droplet of information Alex imparted, rather than drown in my own bleak thoughts. I wrote everything down in my little notebooks, hoping to imprint the places, the tales, the faces. I wanted, I needed to remember each detail. I felt a surge of joy in my heart every time we passed a building that was being restored or a cemetery that was being preserved by the largesse of descendants in the United States, Israel, and other countries. I felt a kinship with all the people I heard about, who made pilgrimages to the towns where their ancestors had once lived, and visited the cemeteries where they lay buried. I didn't know them, but I knew they were helping to keep the ancestral memory alive.

I thought about the parts of the Hebrew Bible that most people skip over: seemingly endless lists of who begat whom. But to me, those lists contain critical information about early ancestors. Everyone knew his or her lineage, which was an essential part of identity. In some tribal cultures today, people still retain knowledge about who they are, based on where and who they came from. It is passed down from generation to generation, as a legacy, through oral stories, weavings, sculpture. It is incised on totem poles and carved in meetinghouses. In Ukraine I felt, more than ever, that without knowing whose shoulders we stand on, we are adrift, rootless, disconnected. We are robbed of part of the meaning of our lives.

In happier times, young Dunca, on the right, with her father.

A van pulls up in front of the former synagogue.

CHAPTER TWELVE -- HINTS IN AMBER

The weather until now had been pleasantly warm but suddenly it became unpleasantly hot. Vitaly rolled down the windows of the van, but we needed air conditioning.

"Vitaly, can you please turn on the air?" Paul asked.

Vitaly didn't answer, so Paul asked again.

"Hey, buddy, we'd like to breathe back here. Can you turn on the air?"

No answer. I saw Paul's jaw tighten, and he clenched his teeth. They sort of looked like fangs. The first time I saw Paul "making teeth" was when we both worked in Hollywood. I had an agent who dressed in black and had a shock of whitish gray in the middle of his black hair. He looked like a skunk. He also acted like a skunk. He showed up at our apartment in Brentwood, a few blocks from where O.J. Simpson lived, and stayed for hours, badgering me, insisting that I make some hefty changes in a script because Whitney Houston was interested in it. "Change this! Change that! Add some color. Do it! Just do it!" He treated writing as though it were flipping pancakes. A few days later, he showed up again, pushing, pushing, wanting changes requested by one of Whitney's people, who, for all I knew, could have been her gardener. My eyeballs rolled around in my head like marbles, but I was compliant.

We worked until midnight, sitting on the sofa of our living room, and I stood up and said I needed a break. "You're just lazy," the skunk said, jumping to his feet.

"Lazy?" A booming voice bellowed. I whipped around and saw Paul standing in the doorway of the room. His fangs were bared. He was "making teeth." He walked towards my agent.

"What's your problem?" el skunko said to Paul.

"I don't have a problem. You do." And without another word, Paul hauled off and decked my agent. Stunned, and sprawled on the floor, skunkie looked up at Paul and said, "I didn't mean it. She's a hard worker. She's not lazy."

At that moment, I would have been thrilled if the floor of the living room had opened up and I had fallen through to a place where I wasn't mortified. I told our friends what Paul had done, and they cheered. They considered Paul a hero. "He did what we all wish we had done," they said.

Vitaly was a far cry from my agent. He nudged the air-conditioning knob a seventeenth of a turn.

"Thanks, Vitaly," Paul said, like a true gentleman. And then he fell asleep. Alex was intermittently nodding off. I was in the back of the car, staring out the window, enjoying the bit of air and the silence.

We drove through the countryside and Alex said, sort of half-heartedly, "We're passing through a town where they have the largest power station in Western Ukraine."

"What's the name of the town?" I inquired.

"Boorshtein."

"STOP THE CAR!" I yelled.

The driver hit the brakes, Paul bolted awake and Alex lurched forward.

To explain why I screamed, I'll have to backtrack a little. Actually, a lot: to my childhood in Queens, New York, and to the two sides of my family.

My mother's parents were Esther and Isidor Kriegsfeld. The former is the subject of this book, and the latter I never knew because he died suddenly at the obscenely premature age of 49. My mother eked out about three terse sentences that described him: he opened a candy store, was short, autocratic, and had been physically and emotionally abusive to my mother. Esther Kriegsfeld was thus widowed, and ran the candy store and somehow supported my mother and her sister. I couldn't pronounce "Kriegsfeld" when I was very little, so I referred to my grandmother as Grandma Tick Tock. After many years of being alone, she married Max Greenspan, a grumpy tailor from Brooklyn who had a huge, stuffed brown bear with an open, cavernous mouth, in the window of his shop. Her name change did not register in my young brain; to me, regardless of her spouse, she was Grandma Tick Tock.

My father's parents were Kate and Kalman Burstein. Grandma Burstein had some great things going for her. She made clothes for our dolls—and my sisters and I were the only kids I knew who had a doll couturier. She also babysat for us on New Year's Eve, when she carefully spooned peach halves out of a can, squirted a ball of whipped cream inside each one of them, and then arranged them on a plate. I always thought it looked like a dish full of eyeballs. She was literate. She had pretty, perky, potted plants on the balcony of her house on Knickerbocker Avenue in Brooklyn. But she had dark hair, thin lips, and she was cold. I never snuggled up to her, and she never snuggled up to me. She had what my parents called a *"farbissine punim"*—a sour puss. She and Grandpa Burstein were separated. The family story was that they wanted to get a divorce, but that was scandalous and verboten at the time, and my father wouldn't permit it. So Kate and Kalman lived separately in the same house, had nothing to do with each other, but were still legally married. I knew she had lost her son Sol—my father's older brother—in a tragic accident. It happened on the day he graduated from the Long Island College of Pharmacy. While he was playing handball, a car ran over him. She certainly had plenty to be miserable about: a deceased child and a botched marriage.

Grandpa Burstein lived in the hall bedroom on Knickerbocker Avenue, estranged from his wife, and then moved in with us when I was young. My parents set up private quarters for him in the basement. He was a mixed bag too. He worked as a house painter— which he pronounced "paintner"—and endlessly played a card game named *pinochle* with a man who lived across the street. They each drank "a cup tea in a glass" and tossed sugar cubes into the glass or, more strangely to my innocent eyes, held a sugar cube between their teeth and sipped the tea through it. My grandfather spoke very little English, so I rarely communicated with him directly. I remember him looking at our bathroom wallpaper, which had images of a mermaid, and pronouncing in Yiddish, "*A maidel mit a veidel*"—a girl with a tail. Once, he accidentally dropped his false teeth in the toilet. Even though he fished them out and sterilized them, he could never wear his choppers again because he pictured them smiling up at him from a full toilet bowl. My mother loved him and said he was very funny. But what did I know? His humor was in Yiddish.

I felt guilty about Grandpa Burstein, because, from the age of three onward, I was convinced I had killed him. It happened this way. Grandpa Burstein liked to play with us kids. One night, when I was about two or three years old, I was sitting on top of the carpeted steps that led to the upstairs. My grandfather came up the steps, and started tickling me. I kicked out in front of me, and he went falling backwards, down the stairs. Sometime after that—it could have been months or years—he died. In my impressionable mind, the two events were linked, and I carried a dreadful secret: I was a murderer.

I also felt exceedingly guilty that I favored Grandma Tick Tock over Grandma Burstein and never dared tell anyone about my preference until one day, when my family was driving to Grandma Tick Tock's house in Brooklyn. I was sitting in the rear seat of our black Chevy, and could no longer hold in my roiling feelings. Pressing my forehead against the front seat, I whispered: "I love Grandma Tick Tock more than Grandma Burstein." I tucked my neck into my shoulders for protection, thinking I would be struck dead on the spot. But either my parents didn't hear me, or they acted as though the car were a confessional booth, and they never mentioned it.

My third source of guilt was that I knew six facts about Grandma Tick Tock's childhood, and zero facts about my grandmother or grandfather Burstein. When I was much older, I reached out to my few extant cousins, to ask if any of them knew about where our grandparents came from, the names of their villages, or anything about how they lived. I heard a few vague stories about my grandmother and it was then I learned that my grandfather was in the Russian army, stationed with other draftees who were mostly Jewish, and they were treated differently from the non-Jewish soldiers. They underwent rifle training and drilling under the watchful eyes and scowling faces of tough sergeants and officers. My grandfather went into battle against the Japanese and surrendered right away. So I clearly do not descend from fighting folk. When the war ended, my grandfather was able to get on an American ship and come to the U.S.A., where he joined his brother Nathan, who was living in Brooklyn. There he took up the trade of house painter and handyman. When he had saved enough money he bought the house on Knickerbocker Avenue and opened a hardware store, which my grandmother ran. And I learned one more fact: my grandfather's name, Burstein, meant amber.

So when Alex declared that we were entering "Boorshtein," which is spelled "Bursztyn" in Polish and is the same as "Burstein," I screamed for the car to stop. I knew that originally the Jews in Eastern Europe had no last names, but were, instead, referred to by nicknames or the names of their professions, like Yankel the Soldier, or Hershel the Cobbler. Beginning several hundred years ago, Jews were forced to take last names, which were then used for legal, commercial, and civic documents. In the nineteenth century, in Russia, officials were assigned the task of giving Jews last names, which were chosen from a variety of sources like remembered origins, professions, geographical features in the areas they inhabited, or the names of the towns where they lived. So it was possible that my grandfather came from the town of Boorshtein, or Burstein.

"Alex, what do you know about Boorshtein?"

He shrugged.

"I think my grandfather came from here. If I had dozed off, we would have missed it. I have to see if there are any clues here. I have to find out."

Alex and Paul sighed, undoubtedly thinking I was chasing wild geese.

"Is there a Jewish cemetery in the town?" I asked Alex.

"Yes, but it's hard to find. It's about half an hour out of our way. And then we have to come back. So that means we lose an hour. If we get lost, more than an hour. And believe me, it's nothing special."

"What else is there? Please, Alex…."

"Well, there's a synagogue. I mean it was a synagogue. Now it's used for something else. I think it's a social center."

"Where is it?"

"Over there, across the road."

I got out of the car, waving for Paul and Alex to follow me. Paul's eyelids were half-closed. Alex was tired. They weren't moving.

Although the street was completely deserted, I raced across

the road to the three-story, white stucco synagogue building as though something were chasing me; actually the thing chasing me was my burning desire to track down my past. And maybe if I found my grandfather's town it would compensate a little for having "murdered" him. And it would get me off the guilt hook of tracking down my mother's ancestors but not my father's.

The moment I arrived in front of the former synagogue, a white van pulled up with two men inside. They looked at me; I looked at them. Since no one in Ukraine seemed to speak English, and Alex wasn't nearby to translate, I was going to keep my counsel but my mouth had a mind of its own.

"Hello. Do either of you speak any English?" I inquired, speaking at a rate of about three words a minute.

"Sure! What do you want?" one of the men replied.

Wow. I pulled the linguistic brass ring.

"I come from here."

"You do?" asked one of the men, and then he began to talk to me in Ukrainian.

"No, no, I mean, I think my grandfather may have come from here. He was Jewish and his name was Kalman Burstein. Does that name ring a bell?"

The two men conferred and then shook their heads.

"It was before our time," they replied. "For a long time there have been no Jews here."

"You mean since the Nazis?"

They shook their heads yes.

"Burstein means 'amber' in Yiddish," I said. My cheeks were flushed with excitement. I had to find something in the town to hang my ancestral-seeking hat on.

"Was there anything in this town in the past that had anything to do with amber?" I asked hopefully.

"Yes," the same man said as he pointed to the building adjacent to the old synagogue. "That was an amber factory."

I was so thrilled I started waving frantically to Paul and Alex who, astounded that a car had driven up on the empty street and I was conversing with the driver and the passenger, ambled towards us. The four men shook hands.

"I hear there is a Jewish cemetery, but it's a long way from town and hard to find," I said to my new acquaintances.

"No, no, it's a few blocks away."

Alex looked sheepish.

"How do we get there? Can you give us directions?" I asked the Ukrainian men.

"Well, why don't we just take you there?"

"I would be so grateful. But tell me, what can I do for you?"

"You can find me a nice American wife."

We all laughed. Alex chatted with the men. Paul focused his camera and photographed them, as proof that this was really happening.

"May I ask you a question?" I inquired of the men. They nodded in the affirmative. "Why did you stop your car in front of the synagogue?"

They looked at each other and shrugged. "I don't know. I'm a truck driver and he's an architect. We were driving and talking and we just….stopped. It's strange. I am not sure why."

Secretly, I knew why. Because I was supposed to meet them.

Because the Finger of Fate had made it happen. I said nothing, but I knew it in my bones.

Paul, Alex, and I crossed back to our car, and followed the white van for a few minutes through back roads until we came to a cemetery. Surprisingly, it was wonderfully preserved. The tombstones were engraved with images: birds, candelabra, a horned animal. The inscriptions were in Hebrew on the front of the stone and Yiddish on the back. I wished I could decipher their meaning, but at least I could read the letters and guess at some of the names and words. In the middle of the cemetery, tombstones had been hauled over and used as supports to prop up a haystack.

"I can't find the name Burstein on any of the tombstones. We're going to leave and I'll never know if my grandfather came from here," I moaned to Paul.

"Look," Paul said to me, as he picked up a white feather that lay at my feet. "It's your ancestors."

I smiled. That's one of the reasons I am married to Paul. Skeptic that he is, he still acknowledges and believes in a certain degree of mysticism, or at least things that are unknowable.

Alex squinted and looked at Paul.

"It's hard to explain," Paul told him. "It started years ago. Wherever Judie goes, she finds a white feather, or a gray feather in her path. She thinks they are signs from her ancestors, kind of an afterlife approval of whatever she's doing at that time."

"Hmmm," said Alex.

"It could be from her grandfather," Paul said.

I just stood there, wide-eyed.

"Maybe her grandfather did come from this village," Paul ventured.

Alex was silent for a long time. "Maybe so," he finally said, with no cynicism whatsoever.

When I got to our hotel that night, I used the computer in the lobby to email my sisters. I wrote breathlessly to tell them that I might have stumbled upon our grandfather's village.

They never replied.

Inside the synagogue where the Baal Shem Tov prayed, healed,
and taught his students.

Man praying at the black-draped tomb of Rabbi Nachman of Bratslov.

CHAPTER THIRTEEN -- VISITING TWO (DEAD) RABBIS

It was over 100 degrees in the car, the air was off, all the windows were closed, and our feet were so swollen from the heat they looked like inflated surgical gloves. Paul's jaw was beginning to tense. He was a step away from "making teeth."

"You must understand that Ukrainians have a pathological fear of cold drafts," Alex whispered to me and Paul. "Our driver, Vitaly, would rather die of heat prostration than turn up the air conditioner. Are you sure you want to drive the extra four hours to visit the rabbis?"

"Sure. What the hell? Who cares if we melt?" Paul replied. "What about you, Judie?"

I thought about it for thirty seconds, then made my decision the way Tevya the Milkman made his in *Fiddler on the Roof*. On the one hand, I'm a secular Jew and do not observe traditional religious practices. On the other hand, I have a passionate interest in the culture, heritage, and history that spawned me, and have definite mystical and spiritual leanings and longings. The rabbis Alex was referring to were mystical, spiritual masters. On the third hand, unfortunately, both rabbis were dead. But, fortunately, their power could reportedly still be experienced at their tombs. On the fourth hand, the great rabbis had enormous impact in the villages, they influenced my grandmother and were part of the context in which she lived. Visiting their tombs would bring me closer to my grandmother and her world. So how could we possibly be in western central Ukraine, so close to the tombs of two world-famous rabbis—the Baal Shem Tov and Rabbi Nachman of Bratslav—and not visit? We had already endured six hours in the car on a searing June day and hadn't expired, so I nodded a sweaty yes.

As we headed towards Medzhybizh, I reflected on what I knew about the Baal Shem Tov—Israel ben Eliezer—the rabbi who began the Hassidic movement in the eighteenth century. Hassidism had great appeal for Jews in Eastern Europe who had suffered decimation in murderous pogroms; grinding poverty; exclusion from the club of learned Torah scholars; and the draconian demands of adherence to 613 rules that governed every aspect of their lives. Most people could comfortably comply with 20, 30, 50 or even 100 rules––but 613?

Hassidism was a great relief, and it rolled across the landscape like a huge ball that gained momentum, gathering followers everywhere it went in Eastern Europe. It offered joy, celebration, and a direct, personal, experiential path to God. According to the Baal Shem Tov, the Creator could be reached not only through Torah study, but through words, deeds, behavior towards others, and everyday actions. It swung open the mystical doors for everyone, not just Torah scholars or those who were literate and educated. Of course the sacred book was important, but there was a deeper, hidden level that could be accessed not only through the head, but through what is arguably the most important organ—the heart. Kindness was valued. Compassion ruled. Intuition mattered. Feelings were not to be pushed away; they could be trusted. It made me think about kindred souls all over the globe today who belong to different religions but feel a void, and are crossing over to paths they feel are more directly spiritual, mystical, and personal, often seeking out a spiritual teacher or guru. The Baal Shem Tov was the revered spiritual teacher and guru to his devoted followers.

Often called the Besht, the eighteenth-century master was humble, lived simply, and was not driven by ego or money. He taught that the Divine was everywhere and in everything; that every person is basically good and can be redeemed no matter what bad things he has done, and that the spirit and sacredness of religion are more important than the form. He spent long stretches of his life alone in the woods, and encouraged his followers to leave behind their suffering and poverty in urban areas, to become sustainable farmers in the country. A very modern thinker, the Baal Shem Tov.

Vitaly—whom we liked and appreciated in spite of his air conditioning flaw—stopped in front of a grassy area that led to a single-story building with white plastered walls, a brown tiled roof, and exposed wooden beams.

"This is the Besht's synagogue," Alex said. "The foundation is original and the building itself was lovingly reconstructed by donors in 2005. Pilgrims come here from all over the world. About twenty to thirty arrive for Sabbath, but many more come on Rosh

Hashanah, the Jewish New Year."

Beyond the synagogue was a long stretch of dense forest. Had the rabbi gone into those woods to meditate, seek communion with Father God and Mother Earth and search for inspiration? I wished he were alive to answer my questions.

I hadn't noticed before, but a gardener was mowing grass near the synagogue. "*Pryvit!*" we called out to him, saying hello in Ukrainian. As we entered the building, I heard someone breathing behind me. I wheeled around, and came face to face with the gardener.

"The Baal Shem Tov prayed at the *bimah*, the place where the Torah was read," he said, inviting me to accompany him to the front of the large room that served as a synagogue. I felt humbled by standing where the great Hasidic master once stood. The gardener suggested I turn around to look at the rough-hewn wooden benches and ledges where the disciples of the famous rabbi prayed and stored their *talitot* (prayer shawls) and other ritual objects. "You have the same view the Besht had," the gardener explained. My imagination ran wild; I could almost see the eager disciples, their eyes wide with hunger for words of wisdom.

He beckoned me to a long, wooden table, and said this was where the rabbi talked to people privately and counseled them. I imagined how powerful it must have been to have face-to-face time with the master. Then he led me to a corner of the room. "This is where the Besht prayed." I followed him as he opened the door to a small side room with a long table and a stove with a hot plate. He invited me to enter. "In this room, he performed the healings for which he was famous." As he said this, the gardener looked me in the eyes. Did he know that I longed for healing, for release from a crippling medical phobia that has plagued me since the time of my father's terrible and rapid death in a hospital when he was 50 years old?

Breaking eye contact with me, the gardener continued. "In his healings, the Besht used faith and herbs. He charged nothing, but the rich gave him money and the poor brought him chickens."

I looked at him quizzically, wondering who he really was. "Are you an official guide here?"

"No. I am the caretaker. I am not Jewish. I have learned by listening to all the experts who have come here. Am I correct in believing that you want to hear more?"

When I nodded so vigorously that my head almost bobbed off my neck, he launched into a condensed biography of the rabbi who was orphaned as a child, widowed when he was in his early 20's, and lived in the forest like a hermit for a decade, learning the language of birds, flowers and all of nature. Then he settled in Medzhybizh, married the town rabbi's daughter, and began his healing work.

The caretaker told me one of the many legends about the Baal Shem Tov. "Once, the rabbi got caught in a swamp. A man helped him to get out, and the Besht was grateful and asked him if he wanted money or health. The man chose health. The rabbi stuck a stake in the earth and a spring came forth. He told the man to drink from that water and he would be healthy. He did, and he was." When he ended the story, he looked at me. Every word he spoke felt pertinent, personal, relevant.

By the time the caretaker finished recounting a few more legends, I was sitting on a wooden bench, rapt. Like the famous Besht, the caretaker was simple, articulate, modest, and showed up at precisely the right moment when he was needed. "In 1760, the Besht assembled his disciples and told them he was going to die soon. He asked them to select water, fire, or blood. They chose fire. Before he died, he gave them a special powder and told them to put it on their houses. When he expired, some of the houses started to burn because of the powder, but when the Besht's coffin passed, the fire went out and had no ill effect on the houses."

And with that, the caretaker finished his compelling mystical narrative and bid us *adieu.*

"Who is he, really?" I asked Alex.

"I don't know. I have come here before, but have never seen him. You are very lucky."

I am lucky, I thought. It's as though everything is unfolding in front of me and all I have to do is show up and pay attention.

We drove for a few minutes to a cemetery, where several tents and tables with half-broken wooden candelabras greeted us. An old toothless man, who happened to be passing by and was the only other visitor in the cemetery, explained that pilgrims had recently come for the Jewish holiday of Shavuot, which celebrates the day God gave the Torah to the ancient Israelites at Mount Sinai. "And you should see how many come for Rosh Hashanah, for the New Year," he added. "Do you come from Ukraine?" he asked me. Startled, I said,

"Yes, yes."

"Welcome," he said. "I thought you looked Ukrainian." Then he disappeared.

"Why did he ask if I came from Ukraine? How could he know?" I asked Alex and Paul.

They shrugged.

"Have you ever been here for Rosh Hashanah?" I asked Alex. He shook his head no.

Unlike the secular New Year, which is often marked by champagne, fireworks, more champagne, more fireworks, and a lot of partying, the Hebrew New Year takes place in the autumn and is the beginning of the High Holidays, a very sacred and significant time of year. It is on Rosh Hashanah that the Book of Life is opened each year. I have told friends of different cultures and religions about Jewish beliefs surrounding the Book of Life, and several have adopted the powerful practices around asking for and obtaining forgiveness.

The book remains open for ten days, and is irrevocably sealed on Yom Kippur. During that period, the fates of the wicked, the righteous, and folks who fall somewhere in between, are determined for the next year. Some will live and others will die; some will perish by fire, and others by water. During this intense period, people are acutely aware of their behavior; they meditate on their actions and can repent for wrongdoings. It is a time to ask for forgiveness from others they have wronged or hurt, whether intentionally or unintentionally. I have found it very moving and beautiful to have someone look into my eyes and say, "Please forgive me if I have knowingly or unknowingly done anything to hurt or offend you." When the ten days are over, the fate for the following year is written, and then, "Bam!" The book is shut. People often say to each other, "May you be inscribed for a good year." The words have great resonance, as everyone wishes to be recorded positively in the book, and to be favored by destiny.

On Rosh Hashanah, a *shofar*, or ram's horn, is blown, and it is traditional to eat apples dipped in honey, which symbolizes a sweet year. It's not difficult to imagine why Jews undertake pilgrimages at this holy, personal, and significant time of year, and why the grave of the Baal Shem Tov is a magnet for spiritual seekers.

We walked past old headstones and Alex pointed to a cluster of white tombs. "Those are the dynasty of the Besht," he explained. We followed him into an *ohel*, or mausoleum, which was crowded with eight tombs. One of them, rounded and constructed of white marble, was inscribed, "*Baal Shem Tov Hakodesh,*" the holy Baal Shem Tov.

A young Hassidic rabbi, with *payot* (sidelocks), dressed in black, prayed quietly at the sacred tomb. His face was radiant and he smiled at us as he explained that he wrote books and articles about the Baal Shem Tov, followed the way of the great rabbi, and that this was his first visit. It was, he said, one of the most important moments in his life. He introduced himself as Yaakov Ben Hanan, and asked if it was okay to share his love of the Besht with us at this holy site. When we nodded enthusiastically, he began to tell us stories of the

Besht, and then he broke into song. "The words are about peace, and all my brothers and sisters," he explained. "I learn from the Baal Shem Tov to have love and peace in my heart for all Jews, even if they don't know the *Torah*. Even if they are secular and non-observant."

Secular and non-observant. Was he talking about me? Were the caretaker and Rabbi Ben Hanan emissaries of the Baal Shem Tov? Why did they show up at precisely the right moment to include, instruct, and even validate me in my life and on my quest for ancestral connection?

We got back into the steaming car and I began to wonder if the Baal Shem Tov's love extended to all humanity. Was it limited to Jews? I thought about the Chmielnicki Cossack murders of 1648-1649. It is estimated that as many as 100,000 Jews were massacred, driving the stake of terror into the hearts of Eastern European Jews. There was also crushing anti-Semitism, and, to make matters worse for *shtetl* dwellers like my ancestors, affluent and educated Jews often didn't want to mingle with their illiterate and impoverished brethren. So the Besht reached out to the Jews around him, in his community, and the villages and towns of Eastern Europe. Regardless of their station, and exquisitely aware of their suffering, he offered them hope, joy, inclusiveness, and love. Were he alive today, I am sure he would have opened his arms and reached out to all sentient beings. I wished I had been among those who experienced the exuberant radiance of his presence.

We drove several hours to Uman, where the Besht's great-grandson, the famous Hasidic master, mystic, and healer, Rabbi Nachman, is buried. We arrived at midnight and, after half an hour, Vitaly, frustrated by the complexity of the warren of streets, found our hotel by asking for a police escort. We schlepped our bags up three floors, and were pleased to find that our accommodation was a spacious suite; the only problem was that it was the one room in the hotel that had no windows and no air. We turned on the cold water in the shower and doused ourselves multiple times during the night. "I am sure that Rabbi Nachman himself couldn't sleep here!" I growled.

I thought about my introduction to the great mystical rabbi about twenty-five years ago, when I listened to a series of tapes about him and his views on healing. He referred to doctors as the "angels of death," and addressed the torment of persistent illness— physical or emotional. When you are sick, it's like there is a sentence on your head. The main difference between this sentence and a prisoner's is that the latter knows how long he will have to spend in prison—five years, ten years, twenty years, but at least he knows when he will be free. When you are ailing, you have no idea of how long it will last. And the only prescription for the seemingly endless suffering is *hisbodedut:* talking *out loud* to God, as though you were speaking to your best friend; it should preferably take place in nature, for one hour a day. Although I told numerous people about it, and it worked for them, I wondered why I had never committed to the practice of *hisbodedut* myself. I could have talked intimately to the Divine, saying I had no idea who He/She was, and questioned whether any religion had a monopoly on reaching Her/Him. I could have expressed thanks for many miracles in my life, and asked for one more. I might have expressed hopelessness and helplessness, shame, frustration and anger about my intractable phobia. Thinking about *hisbodedut,* my life and the rabbi's life, which ended tragically in 1810 when he was 38 and contracted tuberculosis, I fell asleep.

In the light of day, I was stunned by what I found near the tomb of Rabbi Nachman: within the town of Uman, a little Jewish town has grown up. I knew that Christians made pilgrimages to the Holy Land and Muslims made pilgrimages to Mecca. Buddhists may go to Nepal, where the Buddha was born, Bahai travel to Baghdad and *Kumbh Mela,* in the Hindu faith, is a time of pilgrimage and the largest gathering of humans in the world. India is also the site of pilgrimages for Sikhs and Zoroastrians, and, historically, Alexander the Great was said to have interrupted his military campaigns and put the entire military force on hold while he went on pilgrimage to the oracle of Amun in Egypt. Until about 2,000 years ago, Jews made pilgrimages to the temple in Jerusalem three times a year. After the temple was destroyed in 70 C.E. and Jews went into exile, a tradition arose of going to the tombs of Jewish saints and sages, especially on holidays. I had seen remnants of one such pilgrimage at the tomb of the Baal Shem Tov, but this was a permanent, well-organized, year-round phenomenon. Like all the other pilgrimage sites that beckon to pilgrims around the world, the tomb of Rabbi Nachman has great significance to people who are on a spiritual quest, and they often report deriving great benefit from their visits. I wondered if I, too, would have a meaningful, personal experience.

The curb of the steep main street in this Jewish town-within-a-town in Uman is lined with artists and vendors selling Rabbi Nachman-inspired paintings and crafts, and many of the signs are in Hebrew. Bookstores are stocked with books about him and black-cloaked Hasidim—especially Breslov Hasidim, who are his followers—are everywhere. Accommodations and eateries have sprung up to house and feed them.

During the rabbi's lifetime, he gave teachings to his thousands of followers who came from near and far on special Jewish holidays. On the last Rosh Hashanah before his death, he emphasized the importance of the Jewish New Year and told his followers that they should be with him for that holiday. After his death, pilgrimages to the rabbi's tomb on Rosh Hashanah began. The practice continued, although it was greatly restricted and had to go underground during the Bolshevik years, when there was the threat of punishment, imprisonment, and persecution for all religious practices. After the fall of communism in 1989, the practice resumed and today tens of thousands of pilgrims arrive for Rosh Hashanah, where they gather at a lake for ritual purification. Many other pilgrims and visitors come throughout the year to pray, meditate, pay homage, ask for miracles, seek blessings, and have a spiritual experience. A young woman from Israel explained to me in perfect English, "In the synagogue, God is abstract, and hard to reach. There's nothing to see, to touch; you just have to believe. But a tomb is something physical. And inside is one of God's ambassadors. It is a way of getting closer to God. People come here who are very religious yet others are not religious at all.

Even if you have tried to get pregnant for ten years without success, you can come here and have a miracle." I wondered if that was why the young woman had come.

Alex and Paul headed to the men's side of the building that houses the rabbi's tomb, and I walked on a long concrete path lined by what looks like thick, white shower curtains—they block the view to the men's area. I arrived at the entrance to the tomb building; it was dotted with benches and *tzedakah* (charity) boxes. In Judaism, it is a religious and spiritual obligation to assist others by giving them the means to help themselves. My grandmother told me about *tzedakah*, and said it didn't matter how much you gave—dimes, quarters, or dollars; the important thing was to give. Even people who are poor must make contributions, no matter how small. "It's a good feeling in the heart when you give," my grandmother explained. Charity is also a central aspect of Muslim and Christian faiths. It is a way, through religion, to distribute wealth, behave communally, and never forget that others are in need. In fact, the highest form of charity in Judaism is anonymous giving; it obviates shame or obligation in the receiver and self-congratulation, bragging, or feelings of superiority in the giver.

When I opened the door to the building, I saw a playpen for babies, dozens of *tzedakah* boxes in all shapes, sizes, and colors, and bookshelves lined with prayer books; I selected a thin paperback, and smiled when I saw that the cover art was a fiddler on a roof.

The tomb itself was covered in black material with gold Hebrew lettering; on top of it was a protective plastic layer. Prayer requests, written on small pieces of paper, were taped to the top of the tomb. A young Hasidic woman with a baby daughter in her hands sat next to the sepulcher. She must have felt me approaching behind her, because she turned and smiled at me. She was elegantly dressed in a long black skirt and the hair of her raven-colored wig caressed her face and cascaded down her shoulders. Like other Hasidic, Orthodox, and ultra-Orthodox married women, she wore a wig to cover and hide her hair, which might be sexually arousing to men other than her husband.

She held her baby daughter up to the tomb so she could touch it. Another religious woman rocked gently as she read from a prayer book. Then she leaned her head on the tomb, and I heard her soft sobs. I sat down next to them and waited, trying to figure out what a secular woman should do. Suddenly, I heard a male voice say, "Ask. Ask for healing. You can ask as many times as you wish." I turned to look behind me, but no one was there.

I knew exactly what the mysterious voice was alluding to: my phobia, which torments me when I have any contact with doctors or medical settings. I had tried every conventional and unconventional therapy I could find. All I knew was this: before my father died a horrible, premature death, I was fearless. When they were operating on his brain, I was in a state of suspended animation, not fully alive, unable to inhale and exhale normally. The surgeon came out of the operating room to the waiting room, and I ran up to him. "Will my father survive? Please tell me he won't be a vegetable." The doctor was a fine specimen of human warmth. "We cut out a chunk of his brain and we couldn't get the rest. No one has ever survived this." He turned his back on me, strode from the waiting room, and disappeared. That did it for me. My soul collapsed. The haunting began.

I had almost given up on anything helping me, ever, but when I stood at the tomb of Rabbi Nachman, I allowed for the possibility that the afterlife might have a cure for me.

Hesitatingly, I reached out and touched the tomb. My head fell involuntarily onto my chest. I closed my eyes, prayed silently, and asked for help, for a miracle. Was it my imagination, or did I suddenly see a bright purple light in the darkness? I opened my eyes, blinked, then closed them again. The purple light was still there. "Thank you," I intoned. "Thank you."

Before I left the room, a young woman approached me with an outstretched hand, asking for *tzedakah*. I told her I had already made contributions in two boxes. "Please help me," she implored. "I don't have enough money to run my household. Rabbi Nachman will open the gates for you." I gave to her, hoping that indeed, the gates would open.

I rejoined Alex and Paul in the street. Both are very secular. "Did you pray for your herniated disk?" I asked Alex, in a half-joking manner. He quite seriously replied that he had. "And you?" I asked Paul, expecting a funny reply from my very comical husband.

"A man approached me," he said without a trace of irony. "He told me that no matter what I had done in my life that was wrong, the good rabbi would come out of the grave and pull me from the jaw of hell if I said a little prayer. So what did I have to lose?"

The three of us walked in silence to our car. I thought about my grandmother and the phone conversations we had when I was living in San Diego, California, and she was a resident in a retirement facility in Far Rockaway, New York.

"How are you, Gram?" was the way I started each conversation.

"I'm singing and dancing," she replied, which was her ironic way of saying that things weren't great.

"What's wrong, Grandma?"

"The *mishigas kim meir ein*," she sighed. "The craziness has come over me."

I understood what she meant. My grandmother was periodically in the thrall of a psychological and physical affliction. It was hard for her to describe, but I imagined it as a general malaise, a feeling of overwhelm and helplessness, an aura of impending doom and separation from the flow of life. She was easily flustered, and if she took a sip of wine, her face immediately turned the color of *borscht*. Sometimes I think she had a sensation of being shaken, like a snow globe. My mother had her own affliction. When I was a child, I remember being at the circus with my mother, who couldn't bear to look at the aerial acrobats and trapeze artists; they gave her a kind of contact vertigo. When they leapt from one bar to another in mid-air, she bolted from her seat and left for the bathroom. About ten minutes later, a policeman came to our row and asked if we were her family. He informed us that my mother had fainted.

With my father in the lead, we ran from our seats and found my mother in a hallway. She hadn't actually passed out, but she felt as though she were going to. It was most likely a panic attack, which used to be called an anxiety attack. I think it was the beginning of a downhill slide that ended with her unable to get on public transportation. She lay in bed, withdrawing from all but essential activities for more than a year. She went to a psychiatrist at a time when most other people didn't dare mention that word. She was very open about her psychotherapy, and from that time on, anyone who had a psychological problem was sent to my mother for encouragement and support, which she readily provided.

When anxiety diseases were given out, I was next in line. Sometimes I could function very well and sometimes I felt the *mishigas kim meir ein*, the craziness come over me.

From my grandmother, to my mother, to me. So much is passed down from the ancestors. My mother's father had been highly abusive; he beat and punished her. She never dealt with it. She denied its importance, and insisted that it had no impact on her life. Without acknowledgement, she was doomed to repeat it. Without healing, abusers often abuse. Maybe she was acting out an old drama. Of her three daughters, I was most like her, rebellious and spunky. Maybe she did to me what her father had done to her, in a kind of trance from her own past. Perhaps I could return one New Year and ask Rabbi Nachman to open my mother's eyes, so she could let go of her own past. And maybe, if she were healed, then I could be too. Maybe the chain of anxiety had to be broken somewhere. It hadn't happened in the U.S., but maybe in Ukraine, where our roots were?

My feet kept walking along the road in Uman, but my head was in the past, in my grandmother's house in Brooklyn, in the facility where my grandmother lived in Far Rockaway, in my childhood home, in an Oz of wish fulfillment, where things are magically healed and all is right with the world. Where my mother would have had the mother she wanted, and I would have the mother I needed.

"Do you want to come back here some time for the High Holidays?" Paul asked, as though reading my thoughts, which he often did.

As we opened the door to the mobile sauna, I replied, quietly, hopefully, "Yes."

An artist depicts Jewish life in Uman.

A Gypsy mansion in Soroca -Moldova.

The Gypsy Baron of Moldova.

CHAPTER FOURTEEN -- THE JEWS AND THE GYPSIES OF MOLDOVA

Before I left the U.S. for Ukraine, Alex and I exchanged a flurry of emails; he wanted to nail down the itinerary with me so he could reserve hotel rooms. I automatically said yes to most of the places he suggested, without really knowing anything about them. The only time I hesitated was when Alex wrote that two other *shtetl*-seeking clients of his had wanted to extend their search to Moldova, which had a significant Jewish presence, but crossing the border and getting permission had been a hassle and a half and he didn't want to do it again. Moldova? A country I had never heard of? This awakened the Marco Polo in me. I quickly googled and found out that Moldova had been part of the former Soviet Union, and in 1991 it declared its independence. Its history extended back to the Cucuteni-Trypillian people in the Neolithic Age, and included invasion by Goths, Avars, Pechenegs, Cumans and others. I was in ignorant bliss. It was not I, but Marco Polo who wrote back to Alex, imploring him to try once more to cross the border with us into the Republic of Moldova.

He finally acceded, and there we were, several months later, arriving at the border between Ukraine and Moldova. In order to cross it, we had to drive across a bridge that spanned the Dniester River.

145

We were far from alone; long lines of pedestrians were waiting for permission to cross. They pushed and pulled carts that were piled high with cartons containing goods they would sell in Moldova. As we looked around us, we noticed that the signs were all written with the Latin alphabet. Moldovan is a Romanian language, and when the border guard spoke to us, it sounded like Italian. He was a pleasant fellow, nodding agreeably as he examined our papers and waved us forward. Alex was surprised at the ease of the crossing, and we were thrilled to be entering a country we'd never heard of.

As soon as we left the bridge behind we were greeted by moneychangers, who took our dollars and gave us *lei* at an approximate rate of one to one. Then we headed along a walnut-tree-lined road for the city of Soroca. Everywhere we looked, locals sold fruit and vegetables from the backs of their cars and trucks. The area used to be the fruit garden of the Soviet Union, but since the collapse of the latter it's become more difficult to export to Russia, and the market is greatly reduced.

We drove past horses and donkeys that grazed in the fields and waved to men driving horse-drawn carts and goatherds shepherding their flocks. About an hour later, we arrived in Soroca and were greeted by clumps of apartment buildings and a large sign that read: "Soroca is our common house." Further along the main road were characterless government buildings and then a surprising sight: extravagant mansions that looked like homes I used to see in Beverly Hills.

"Are these the houses of local Jews?" I asked Alex.

"No," he replied. "These are the homes of Gypsies."

"Gypsies? When did they come here? Where did they come from? What do they do for a living? How do they afford such houses?"

Alex shrugged.

"Do they call themselves Gypsies, or Roma or Tinkers?"

Alex grinned. "I knew you would have a million questions, and I think you can get answers from the Gypsy Baron."

"How do we meet him?"

"I have some ideas. In fact, I am going to his house to make the request tonight."

"Please….yes……do you think he'll agree to see us?"

At that moment, an older Gypsy woman who was missing several teeth smiled at me, and I smiled back. She took my right hand and held it in hers.

"You are good to people and have a good heart," she said. "Because you are good to people, you have good fortune. You will have money and success and you will make an impact on peoples' lives," she told me.

She went on and on about what a stellar person I am, and how fortune smiles on me. And then she asked for a little money. I gave her some, and she asked for more. "It was a really long fortune," she said, "and I told you a lot of things."

I squeezed her hand goodbye, but didn't give her more money. Then a Gypsy woman with gold teeth called to us.

"What country are you from?" she asked.

"The United States."

"Are there Gypsies in the United States?"

"Yes. Yes, there are."

She smiled broadly, her gold teeth gleaming in the magic hour just before sunset. I smiled back at her, and waved.

We continued walking down the street, gaping at mansions with dollar signs on the gates, Greek columns, statuary, and leaping horses. Alex explained that the town had erratic electric power and water, so even though a house might be lavish, the owners must still get water from a hand-cranked well. We passed by an abandoned former synagogue with its stucco façade and brick-framed windows.

"Are there still Jews here?" I asked, hoping there were people who remained from the ancient Jewish community.

Alex nodded. I wasn't prepared for his answer. "Yes, there are Gypsies and Jews. And there is an informal solidarity between them. The country was occupied by Romania, who collaborated with the Nazis. Jews and Gypsies both suffered forced labor, internment, and mass murders in concentration camps."

Alex spoke very quickly, and I tried to take in every word he was telling us. Suddenly, he stopped in front of the Baron's house. Two armored Russian limos were half-buried in his front yard. Alex said the Baron told him that they had been used in Soviet times by Russian apparatchiks, and one of the cars belonged to the First Secretary of the Communist Party of Moldova.

"Why does the Baron keep these cars?" I inquired.

"To show that he is rich and important."

"Alex, please ask if he'll receive us. I want to find out if there is a historical connection between Gypsies and Jews and if that's why they live in the same town. I want to meet a man with Russian limos in his yard. He sounds intriguing...."

"Later. I'll come back later."

We walked on and Alex pointed to a building in a state of disrepair. He said it had been a synagogue. Then it was turned into a movie theatre and was now for sale. I had a sinking feeling that the story behind the second synagogue was the same as the first, and that it was related to the Holocaust.

We stopped at the Ethnographic Museum, wandering past farm implements, embroidery, textiles, beehives, wicker furniture, and carpets. I stopped in front of an icon of Abraham and Isaac, at the time of the latter's binding in preparation for his sacrifice, as it is described in the Hebrew Bible. God was testing Abraham by asking him to sacrifice what was most precious to him—his son. It was a rare image because Isaac was praying. He seemed to know the terrible fate that awaited him at his father's hands. Abraham, the patriarch, was touching Isaac's arm with great tenderness. It was the first time I had ever seen an image of Abraham expressing affection towards his son. After the binding of Isaac, even after an angel intervened and stopped Abraham from killing his son, there was no mention of what happened between the two. For the rest of the Abraham and Isaac story, the son never spoke to his father again directly. In this icon, I could feel the possibility for some healing between them before Abraham died. It was the kind of healing I craved in my own family, which has never taken place. I felt like Isaac, almost sacrificed on the altar of a parent's twisted needs. Ostensibly, Abraham was following God's orders, and the latter was testing him and his faith. My mother had a different excuse. She was acting out her pain on me, as her father had acted out his on her. I wondered how far the cruelty went back through the generations.

Alex then took us to the cement building that housed the 204-year-old synagogue of Soroca. It was a great relief to find a synagogue that was not an abandoned ruin. We walked around to the back of the building where the exterior was adorned with a Jewish star. Next to the synagogue was a light blue gazebo with two Jewish stars, used for parties, and for rest. Alex waved at three members of the congregation who came to meet us: Inna, Liova and Arkady. As soon as the introductions were over, I blurted out that I was on a pilgrimage to find the place my grandmother left behind and that I would be grateful for anything they could tell me about the world they came from because I suspected it was similar to my grandmother's.

They were friendly and open and said they would willingly answer my questions, and tell me a little about their lives. Before the Second World War, Jews made up more than 50 per cent of the city's population and Soroca had 22 synagogues. In my bones, I knew what they were going to say next. The Jewish community was devastated and decimated by the Nazis. Some Jews were deported, others left with the Soviet Army; many were sent to extermination camps. Their synagogue was closed in 1940, and during the Soviet period it was used as a gym or sports hall.

We followed the three of them into the synagogue, which was a large, makeshift room about the size of a gym. I felt moved and sad to see how reduced the once-thriving population was. In the United States, we had never known such loss and tragedy.

"Survival," I said quietly.

"Excuse me?" Inna asked.

"Survival. It is a miracle you survived," I murmured.

Rows of chairs lined the periphery of the room. The *bimah*, or pulpit, was in the center of the room, and eternal lights lined the *aron hakodesh*, or Holy Ark, where three *Torah*s were kept. Arkady said the pulpit was only used for High Holidays—Rosh Hashanah and Yom Kippur—and it was there the Torah was read. Next to the *bimah* was a smaller pulpit, which was used for prayers during the rest of the year. Upstairs, and visible through a window that looked like a projector room in a movie theatre, was the place where women used to pray, according to the separation of the sexes mandated by Orthodox Judaism. Today, men and women sit together. The congregation gets together for Passover, which is celebrated in the synagogue, instead of individual homes. "The hall we are in is used by religious people. There is a separate hall for secular Jews," Inna explained. "Are you surprised?"

"I sure am."

"It's like the old joke," Paul said to me in an aside, "three Jews, four synagogues. One you go to. One you wouldn't go to. The third where they wouldn't accept you. And a fourth where you wouldn't go even if they asked you. One small synagogue, two separate halls. Of course."

I smiled inwardly. Paul was right. It's axiomatic that Jews are feisty, independent, with many ways to be Jewish—from ultra-Orthodox to secular, to agnostic, to embracing a variety of other religions, philosophies and lifestyles. It is true in the United States, and it is clearly true in Moldova.

I picked up one of the prayer books. It was in Hebrew with Russian translation. In their homes, the first language they learned was Russian, so that explained the translation. Only Inna grew up speaking Yiddish.

I asked our three hosts questions about their past, and what they remembered from their childhoods. I wanted to connect to the way things were, the way they were in the world my grandmother knew.

"When I was young, my parents sent me to the *shochet*—the ritual slaughterer—to buy kosher chickens. We used kosher plates and utensils. It was different from now," Liova reminisced.

"My grandmother used special dishes for Passover," Inna chimed in. "And there was a *mikvah*, a ritual bath, but that's gone now."

Their memories were fading. They were a link to the past, and already that past was dim. It added even more urgency to my trip, and to my desire to go anywhere, meet anyone, who could connect me to the reality of life in the *shtetls* before it was all gone.

"There are still remnants of the past," Inna said, as though reading my thoughts. "We have a cemetery that dates back to before the Second World War. And two monuments to the Holocaust. Samuel Bronfman, the liquor magnate and philanthropist, originally came from this area. He left at the end of the nineteenth century. His grandson Matthew Bronfman sponsors a lot of the teaching we receive. They help us a lot." I thought about the difference between Samuel Bronfman, who left Eastern Europe and became wildly, remarkably successful, and my grandmother, who still had one foot in the shtetls when she came to America, and was never remarkable to anyone but me.

As we spoke, my eyes scanned the room and settled on a deer painting. "It's a kosher animal," Liova explained, "and it's also a symbol of generosity." Both attributes were news to me. I knew that the deer was sacred to many native people, but I had no idea it was such a potent symbol for my ancestors.

My brain expanded to take in everything I was learning. I felt as if every detail was significant, no matter how small. All of it brought me closer to my ancestors, and to Minkowitz.

"Can you tell me what you ate, growing up?"

They became very animated and said that the Jews of Soroca originally came from Poland so they ate, and still eat, *gefilte* fish, *chrain* (horseradish), kasha, kasha *varnishkas* (kasha with different shapes of pasta added), and *kigel* (noodle pudding). They even made *matza kigel* for Passover.

"I ate all of it!" I gushed. "My grandmother and my mother made *kigel*, although we called it *kugel*. How about *hamantaschen* for Purim? Do you know that? It's like a triangle-shaped pastry that can be filled with poppy seeds, prunes, all kinds of things."

"Yes! Of course we know *hamantaschen*!"

"*Latkes*—potato pancakes—for Hanukah?"

"Yes!"

"*Shmaltz*? Chicken fat?"

"Yes, yes. With onions. And they even make kosher wine and sell kosher food in Kishinov. They have a *mikvah* there too."

I was there, I was really there, connecting to people who ate what we ate, who grew up the way we did, celebrated the same holidays we did. The only difference was that most of them had been annihilated because they were born into a religion. The dead could have been teachers and social workers, doctors and lawyers, singers and mechanics. Instead, their bones were charred in ovens and they were gassed in showers.

"Did you lose family members to the Nazis?" they asked me.

"No. I didn't."

What I didn't say was that the Holocaust was not emotionally real or accessible to me. It happened before I was born. In Europe. It was one of the enduring horrors that humans perpetrated on other humans. It was unthinkable. Unimaginable. My brain and my heart couldn't understand it.

"Come, look," Arkady said, interrupting my reflections. We followed the trio upstairs to the social hall, museum and library, and I looked out the window and saw a Gypsy mansion with a shimmering gold dome.

"Jews and Gypsies," I mused. "Is there a historical connection between you?"

Our hosts shrugged and said they didn't know. Alex said he didn't know either.

"But I think the gold dome on the Gypsy house looks like Jerusalem," he added.

"Do you…do the Jews here live in palaces like the Gypsies?" I asked our hosts.

They laughed and said no, they didn't live in palaces, and they weren't sure where the money came from to build the mansions, but they maintain good relations with the Gypsies. The two groups get along just fine. But the Jews live in much more modest homes.

"I hardly live in a mansion. I don't have a lot of money. I'm a pensioner," one of the trio explained. "I teach music. Actually, I teach music teachers how to teach music. I am the only Jewish member of the university staff, so they treat me well, out of respect. You see, in the past, almost all the faculty was Jewish. It's different now."

I grew very quiet. The Holocaust had come up again. It was always there, always part of the reality of the Jews. I tried hard to penetrate the reality behind our hosts' words, and to imagine what it was like to be part of a community that was almost obliterated. To be a living testimony to what was, and to carry the memory of that world inside.

"How did your family survive? I asked in a whisper. "How did they make it through the Nazi and Soviet times?"

"My family managed to go to Eastern Ukraine. My mother's family survived in a ghetto. My grandfather worked with tin, on heating systems, and this profession helped him to survive in Soviet times. During those days, we were afraid to talk about what happened during the Nazi period. There was a lot of fear. Look, on the wall are two prayers for the Soviet Union because they allowed us to re-open the synagogue. Some people really helped us. One of our *Torah*s was saved by non-Jewish Moldovans during the war."

"All of us have relatives in Israel," Inna added. "There's a Soroca diaspora there."

The three told us that the congregation today has 120 members. They have no rabbi, no kosher food and they "sort of" keep the Sabbath, driving on the holy day and taking care of life's necessities. A man reads from the Torah and says the prayers. About 30 of the members have a Jewish maternal line, which is the formal definition of who is officially recognized as a Jew. The others are either mixed marriages, or they are descended from Jews on their fathers' side.

"Do you feel safe here?"

"Yes, we feel secure," they said. "Our life here is quiet and pleasant."

"You have been through so much. I am so sorry for what happened here. And yet you move forward and go on. I have learned a lot from you. Thank you."

"How do they do it?" I wondered. How does one break the shackles of the past? I had worked so hard on it, but I still trailed chains behind me, and their clinking unnerved me.

"We must go now, "Alex said, adding to me, in an aside, "I have to meet with the Gypsy Baron to see if he will receive you. I know he'll have a lot of answers for you."

Paul and I hugged our hosts good-bye, thanking them again for taking the time to visit with us. Then we waited in the hotel for Alex to return. When he did, his mouth was turned down into a frown. It seemed that the Gypsy Baron was tired and in a foul mood. He wouldn't meet with us.

I was sorely disappointed. So was Paul.

"There's no way....?" he asked Alex.

"Well," he replied, "let's have a good night's sleep and maybe the Baron will have a good night's sleep as well. I'll try again in the morning."

True to his word, after breakfast Alex headed off to the home of the Gypsy Baron ...with us in tow. Once again, we arrived at the house, and looked at the two half-sunken limos. This time we noticed that there was a bullet hole in the windshield of the car that belonged to the First Secretary of the Communist Party of Moldova, who probably missed a near-rendezvous with death.

"You wait here in the yard," Alex instructed us. "I will go into the house to speak to him."

We paced around the yard, accompanied by crowing roosters and chickens. At length, we were joined by two turkeys and a mangy dog. Clothes dried on a long clothing line, along with a Mickey and Minnie Mouse bath towel. There was an outhouse. We looked up at the Baron's large, three-story, brick house. Carpets, newly washed and slung over railings, hung out to dry on each of the three floors.

It was searingly hot, and there was no shade in the yard. Our clothes were drenched in perspiration. There was no sign of Alex. After a while, a young woman in a sequin housedress came out of the mansion. She didn't smile, but she wasn't hostile. She approached us without much interest, as though we were flies or gnats, and motioned for us to sit down on chairs. Then she went to a covered alcove near the clothesline, pulled out a hose, turned on the water, and pointed it towards our feet, presumably to cool us down. Pretty soon, our feet were in a puddle. When she wasn't looking, we tried to move the hose to spray on our ankles or shins, but the hose snaked wildly and we couldn't tame it. So we directed it back to our feet, and sat there awkwardly, wet and waiting. At one point I glanced up, and I saw the young woman in sequins looking furtively at me. It occurred to me that maybe she had a mistrust of strangers. Perhaps her fear of outsiders, like the fear of many Jewish people, was grounded in the grinding prejudice and persecutions of the past. I knew her people were stereotyped, as mine were. The general perception was that Gypsies can't be trusted, so maybe she felt the same way towards non-Gypsies: they are not to be trusted. What did I know about Gypsy history?

About 15 minutes later, Arturo, the Gypsy Baron for all of Moldova, drove up in a beige car, and shook our hands. He looked like Santa Claus, with a big, bushy white beard and twinkling eyes. He was attired in casual, contemporary clothes: beige slacks and a short sleeve shirt. Then he went into the house and spoke to Alex. Alex came out and told us that the Baron wanted $100 to talk to us. We said this was not acceptable to us, and that, as journalists, we didn't pay to talk to people. Alex went back into the house to relay our refusal. We figured that the Gypsy Baron, like the young woman in the sequin dress, probably didn't trust us. Maybe he doubted we were journalists. We were getting ready to leave when Arturo came outside with his grandson Vasily, and sat down next to us. We smiled broadly, said we appreciated his time, and then asked questions, listening intently to his thoughtful and intriguing replies. He said he was a linguist and historian, so we covered a broad range of subjects. As we spoke, his daughter came out from the house and served us walnuts, cognac, and tea.

"Do you prefer the name Gypsy?" I inquired.

"We're called by different names in different countries. Tinker is closest to the true meaning, but saying Gypsy is fine."

"Do the Gypsy traditions date to pre-Christian times?"

"Yes," he replied. "Around the year 200 C.E., the Gypsies accepted Christianity. They were Buddhists before. Alex says you are Jewish…."

I nodded. He looked me directly in the eyes.

"Do you know why the Jews wandered in the desert for 40 years?"

I shook my head no, knowing that he wasn't asking for an obvious response.

"The Jews and Gypsies both spoke Aramaic, so we share a

common ancient language. Gypsies were in all the old Aramaic lands, and spoke Aramaic until the Pharaoh expelled Moses and the Jews to the desert. Then they evolved their own language that only they could understand, but before that, we shared the same language."

My eyes opened wide in surprise.

"The Jews with Moses were ancient escapees from India," he continued. "The Gypsies were in those territories first. They came from India with the Jews and settled in Egypt with them. Think about it: why did Pharaoh start to hate and expel the Jews? Because they became so rich with gold and silver that Pharaoh disliked it. They were newcomers in the Pharaoh's land, but they became richer than he was! The Jews were very close to us. Very close. Only the languages we used changed."

Before I could react, he wished me and Paul health and long life and then drank cognac with us, and started peppering his talk with Yiddish expressions. "Jews talk about having a *Yiddishe kup*, a Jewish head. The Gypsies say 'a head with gold and silver.' Like the Jews, we can't live without music and humor. And we also need gold and fun. We Gypsies love gold like you do."

"I don't care about gold," I said.

"Actually, you see that I wear no gold, even though I am a jeweler. Did you know that Gypsies were the first military industrial complex? They were blacksmiths for kings all over the world. We forged their weapons."

We toasted to Jews and Gypsies and drank cognac for a long moment in silence. Then Arturo continued: "The Jews learned to read and write two to three thousand years ago. But the Gypsies had no interest in reading and writing. Gypsies did physical work. Jews were craftsmen and worked in construction. The Gypsies did this as well."

I brought up the subject of Gypsy stereotypes, and how people accused them of stealing. Paul winced. Alex winced. But Arturo didn't.

"We cannot reject the historical truth," he said. "Many nations came from us. The negative stereotypes persist and will persist. We did steal. That is true. It is also true that others were jealous of us because we were clever. Good and bad always exist. The stealing by Gypsies is the legacy of Satan. Gold and diamonds will not save the world. Only the nobility of humans will. I try to teach only good. Our people should get more education. To my great sadness, my Gypsy nation still lives in feudal times. There should be mandatory secondary education. Many Gypsies go abroad to earn money, and they leave here without education."

"Do you mind if I ask you about where the money comes from to build such incredible mansions?"

Alex and Paul slouched down in their seats, mortified. But Arturo sat up proudly.

"Most of the money comes from trade," he said. "Not from stealing. I gave orders to the Gypsies here—don't steal, rob, or deal with dope. Just go and earn money. Trade was banned in Soviet times. Now they can trade. You saw people crossing the bridge when you came. They trade *shmatas* and foodstuffs. I am proud of the houses here. There is competition to see who can build the best house.

The houses are built by Gypsy architects. Many do not have formal education. There is a natural capacity among Gypsies, and it goes back to Byzantium and India. Kurds are Gypsies. So are Azerbaijanis, Assyrians, and Chechens. They are Gypsies who remained in Asia and the Caucasus. Others moved here. The largest settlement was in Buda and Pest. The Berbers are Gypsies of the desert. There are many Gypsy words in the languages of the world. Do you know that vendetta comes from the Gypsies? So did 'an eye for an eye.'"

I tried to write down every word Arturo spoke, hoping I could read my own cognac-soaked handwriting and think about what he said later. It was intense conversation peppered with laughter, walnuts, more cognac, and Yiddish expressions.

Arturo's wife appeared at the door, and he introduced her as Lyddia. "She is a *gute balebusta*," he said in Yiddish, referring to her excellence as a homemaker. "Come inside, come see our house."

We followed him inside to the kitchen, where he explained that they all slept there, near the ceramic stove, to keep warm.

I knew, instinctively: This is how my grandmother's family slept in Minkowitz. No one had to tell me. I just felt it in my bones.

Arturo's daughter was curled up and sleeping, but our voices didn't seem to disturb her. I looked around the room and saw two accordions, icons, carpets, and weavings of the Madonna and Jesus.

"We have to go," Alex whispered to me, and I nodded and told Arturo that we had to cross the border and continue our trip in Ukraine.

"*Zei gezint*," he said in Yiddish as we left. Go in good health.

He pronounced it exactly the way my grandmother did.

As we drove back towards the border between Moldova and Ukraine, I tried to process what we had just heard. I couldn't even remember what language we had spoken—bits of Yiddish, Hebrew, German, English, maybe French. Did Alex translate? I couldn't recall. I had just left Arturo, and already I couldn't remember. And why had he decided to spend so many hours with us when he first refused? It was as though I craved answers to questions, and he showed up to check us out, and then decided to supply the answers. I only knew two things for sure. First, that the Jews had such an impact on Moldovan life and culture that it was natural for a connected, intelligent man like Arturo to speak Yiddish. Even though so few Jews were left, Arturo's use of Yiddish helped to keep their memory, history, and cultural legacy alive. And second, I was grateful that Arturo chose to speak to us and to share with us what he and his Gypsy people think and believe. The Gypsies suffered like the Jews suffered. The Gypsies were victims of the Nazis like the Jews were.

The culture my grandmother came from kept expanding before my eyes. I needed to keep seeing, learning, feeling, before I arrived at her *shtetl*. I knew that everything I was experiencing would make the visit richer, deeper, more significant, and would give me insight into the world I originally came from—the world she left behind.

Rabbi Noah Kofmansky of Chernivtsi.

CHAPTER FIFTEEN -- KNOWLEDGE IN THE BONES

It was relaxing to look out the window as we drove through the countryside back in Ukraine. Along the road, vendors sold mushrooms and brooms. The fields were dotted with haystacks. Several hundred years ago, merchants, traders, and travelers probably saw the same timeless sights. I smiled as I pictured a man on his way home, stopping to buy his wife a new broom or a small basket of fresh mushrooms.

After several stops in small towns, we arrived in Chernivtsi (Chernowitz), which has a population of 350,000, is known for its tolerance, and includes a multi-cultural mix of Ukrainian, Gypsy, Jewish, Russian, and Romanian inhabitants. The eighteenth- and nineteenth-century architecture looked decidedly European.

Alex walked us through the old Jewish section, precariously placed near the riverbank and subject to mudslides. The houses were eclectic in style, and included a range of shapes and sizes that were pleasing to the eye. We passed several synagogues, a very large house that belonged to the rabbi, and the Jewish hospital next to it. Alex said that in Ukraine it was rare to see intact Jewish buildings that had not been destroyed. I acknowledged that the Nazis and Soviets were really efficient machines of mass destruction. What the former began, the latter finished. I tried to imagine what life would have been like if they had applied their astounding organizational skills to the betterment of their inhabitants.

"From what I hear, there are a lot of superstitions from the old days that still remain here," Alex commented, once again interrupting my reveries.

My ears pricked up and our guide had my full attention. "You mean when you walk with someone in the street, you shouldn't be separated by obstacles in your path?"

Alex nodded.

"And if you forget something once you leave the house, you shouldn't go back in?"

"I think so."

"What other superstitions do you remember, Alex?"

"Carrying empty barrels means that you will have misfortune."

"I never heard of that one."

"Throw salt over your shoulder if you spill it," Alex said.

I smiled. I knew about the salt. And I also now knew for sure where my grandmother and mother's superstitions had come from. They weren't limited to Minkowitz, but were spread out across western Ukraine, and probably beyond. It was, for me, another connection to the land in which we were traveling.

"I would like to take you to a Jewish cemetery that wasn't destroyed. It's the best preserved one in Ukraine, and is still used today," Alex said.

At the cemetery, he led us to a large *ohel*, or shrine, where *tzaddikim*, or righteous sages, are buried in stone tombs. Next to it was a small *ohel*, where a revered rabbi is interred. On a metallic stand, worshippers had placed candles, and on the black wall of the shrine, they had scrawled prayer requests in chalk. One was from a mother, who pleaded for a mate for her son. I wondered if the son knew that his mother was praying for him, and, if he didn't, would he be mortified by her otherworldly intervention?

The tombstone of the rabbi was inscribed with gold lettering, befitting a man of high stature. In the world my grandmother came from, revered rabbis—known as *rebbes*—were honored in this life and the *olam haba*, the world to come.

Although I am non-observant, I always wondered what it was like to be in the company of one of the great, inspirational *rebbes* who once illuminated the landscape of Eastern Europe. I found out late one Friday night in Israel, in the ultra-Orthodox section of Mea Shearim, in Jerusalem. Hundreds or perhaps thousands of men, clad in black frock coats and black or fur-trimmed hats, and women dressed modestly in long-sleeved clothes, come to attend weekly Sabbath "*tishes*" with the particular *rebbe* they follow. The men sit downstairs, close to the beloved *rebbe*, and the women sit upstairs. There is great joy as the adepts sing *niggunim*, or religious songs that are based on repetitive sounds rather than lyrics.

During the course of the *tish*, the *rebbe* eats a Sabbath meal, surrounded at a long table by his students and followers. He presides like a king, and when he is finished eating, the adepts reach for his crumbs, devouring them like holy morsels.

I was in Hasidic heaven, fascinated by the *tish* that carried me back to Minkowitz and the *shtetl* milieu of my grandmother. I felt blessed to be able to witness a bit of ancient *shtetl* life transplanted to modern day Israel. It was deep, powerful, devotional, and exotic, just as I always believed it to be.

That night, a Hasidic rabbi explained to me why Jews leave prayer requests—in some cases, even faxing their prayers to printers at the *rebbe*'s gravesite if they live far away—at the tombs of their *rebbes*. The latter are believed, because of their holiness, faith, and fine character, to have access to the Divine. Their followers do not pray to the *rebbes*, but they pray for the *rebbes* to intercede on their behalf so that God will grant them favors.

Standing near the tomb of the *rebbe* in the Chernivtsi cemetery, I once again felt privileged to be in contact with my grandmother's world, and marveled at the faith of followers who believed their *rebbes* continued to serve them in the *olam haba*.

As I thought about the *rebbes*, Paul was snapping photos of the tombs. He walked by me and whispered in my ear, "Does this remind you of the *tish* in Mea Shearim? We're actually in the place where that *rebbe* culture came from!" I grinned like a crescent moon. Paul wasn't obsessed like I was, but he was connecting in his own way to the land we both came from.

Alex led us to a large brick *ohel*, where the bodies of the dead were meticulously prepared for burial and last prayers were made. Then Paul and I wandered through the cemetery, gazing at headstones, commenting on symbols and ornamentation. The size and the opulence of some of the tombs were evidence that the Jews lived well in this area. It had, at different times, been part of the

Ottoman Empire, then Romania, Austria, and Russia. Alex said that there had been a large contingent of secular and successful Jews.

"Do you feel anything special among the tombs here?" I asked Paul.

"Not really. Do you?"

"I can admire the headstones, but I find it hard to be moved among the tombs of the wealthy."

Paul nodded his agreement.

Our people came from poverty, and everything about their material lives, as I imagined it, was simple. They came from the earth and returned to the earth, surrounded by tears and ritual observances, remembered by plain stones that recorded their names, dates, and perhaps a quote or testimony about their having been a person of valor.

"Are you ready to go?" Alex asked. When we nodded, he said, "I thought you might be interested in meeting someone who can tell you what life was like here after the Nazis, under the Soviets. You said you want the whole picture, right?"

We drove to Central Synagogue, one of the few houses of worship that miraculously remained open during both the Nazi and Soviet periods. It wasn't officially registered as a synagogue, so it remained under the official radar. The exterior of the small Orthodox synagogue is made of tile and brick. The dominant colors are blue and white, with brown, decorative pillars surrounding the windows. A dome crowns the synagogue. Inside, on the main floor, is a small section where a *minyan*—the ten adult males required for many ritual observances—gathers to pray. The benches are dark brown and a brown stove provides heat. The *aron hakodesh*, or Holy Ark, is covered with a burgundy velvet curtain. The space is simple, unpretentious, the way I imagined a tiny *shtetl* synagogue to be. I am sure that my male ancestors prayed in very similar spaces. They thanked God for the little they had, and in times of need, probably prayed more fervently, swaying back and forth with intensity, asking for health for a child, money to buy food for the Sabbath, or safety from pogroms.

The main chapel is much more expansive and is decorated with murals of the Holy Land. The men sit below, and the women pray from a balcony. The Orthodox separation of genders is supposed to ensure that attention is on prayer and not on the opposite sex. When men and women are not together, they are free to focus on their spiritual, rather than physical, selves. On the ceiling of the chapel are images of deer and lions. Since arriving in Ukraine, and on our brief excursion to Moldova, we learned that animals often symbolized family names; the deer was Hirsch, the wolf represented Benjamin, the rose was Blume and the lion was Loeb. As far as I knew, the only link my ancestors had to the animal kingdom was eating chicken on Friday night, when they could afford it.

My musings were interrupted by the arrival of Noah Kofmansky, the rabbi. He sported a white beard and his eyes were limpid and gentle. He was generous with his time, and agreed to tell us his personal story. "My grandfather was a rabbi," he began, "but my father was not allowed to be a rabbi in Soviet times. Things were difficult economically, and my grandfather told my father, 'Cut your beard and start working.' And so he did, working to support the family. We were exiled to Siberia after the war, along with 20,000 Jews. I became a rabbi only after the collapse of the Soviet regime and the independence of Ukraine. During Soviet times, no one wanted to be a rabbi here. It was too dangerous. The scholars held *minyans* here, but there was no official registration of rabbis or of the synagogue.

"I was a small boy in Siberia," he continued. "My parents were educated and smart. My mother knew herbal medicine and that is how we survived. She was like a doctor."

"You are Orthodox," I observed. "I wonder what your family did to eat kosher food in Siberia."

"We tried to stay kosher by not eating meat; that was our way," he explained. "Times are very different now. In our synagogue there is a *minyan* every day and on the High Holidays there are too many people for the synagogue to hold. Many have to stand outside. There are about 1,200 Jews in town, plus others who don't register as Jews.

"As for myself, I am a solid-state physicist and I am working on how to reconcile physics and Judaism. Several decades ago, I had an idea about using a beam to destroy life, while leaving buildings intact. Then it was reported that the Soviets were accused of using a beam to destroy satellites. I had a dream where a huge man stood over me, and he had a long, white beard. 'What are you doing this for?' he asked me. 'You can do better for yourself in life!' I got scared, and moved away from this line of investigation.

'"Now I am working on a project to create a large memorial in the center of the city in the Jewish quarter. The Romanians and Nazis had a plan to remove Jews from here and ship them to death camps. We must always remember those who came before us."

We could easily have spent another hour or two talking to Rabbi Kofmansky about Siberia, ancestors, and physics, but Alex said we had much to do, that it was time to leave. The rabbi offered a blessing to me before we departed and it resonated in my bones: "Be prudent and wise. Have patience and tolerance in everything you do and you will prosper. I wish you health and success."

It was stirring to hear the words from someone who had been victimized by intolerance, and whose family had exercised enormous patience when they were in Siberia. I pondered what the word "prosper" meant. I didn't think it referred to money. When I worked in Hollywood, I made a lot of money, and I was surrounded by people who made half the GNP of some emerging nations. But I never felt prosperous, nor did I think of the others as prosperous. Almost everyone lived in fear—that a deal would fall through, that you'd be fired, that a producer or director or star would drop out of your project, that your agent would dump you, that your script would languish in development hell and your career would go cold. They spent lavishly in restaurants with *auteur* chefs and on impeccably tailored Armani clothes. "I'm having such a problem," the Vice President at a major studio once said to me. "I just can't find a decent suit for under three thousand dollars." They drove or were driven in

Ferraris, Mercedes and BMWs, which they leased and changed every few years, or sometimes annually. They bought houses in Malibu or the Hollywood Hills, but there was always the looming threat of losing it all. That one day you'd wake up, like Cinderella after the ball, and it would all be gone—the coach, the white horses, the pomp, the prince. Prosperity was an inner acquisition, the flourishing of the self, the expanding awareness of the great gift of being human. It was a call to act prudently and with wisdom—looking at the big picture, not getting caught up in the trivialities of everyday life. I thanked the rabbi vocally and in my heart.

Before leaving Chernowitz, we stopped at the building that houses the History and Culture Museum of Bukowynian Jews (the region we were in is known as Bucovina). We learned that there had been a ghetto in the city, and in an area where 5,000 people lived before the war, 45,000 forcibly displaced Jews resided. Approximately 50 per cent of the Bukowynian Jews—and Chernowitz was the most important community in the area—were killed, transported, exterminated, or died of hunger. The local Mayor, a Gentile man named Popovici, became an ardent defender of the Jews; he stopped the deportations and helped approximately 20,000 Jews return to their plundered homes. I hoped he would forever be remembered as a man of great valor, a light to the nations, and a hero.

I also learned that the problems for Jews in Bucovina started long before the Second World War. Romania occupied Chernowitz in 1918, when there was a marked rise in anti-Semitism. Jews were second-class citizens, although they were allowed to continue their theatre, newspaper, and synagogue observances. In 1940, there was a wave of pogroms; Jews were forced to wear a yellow star and were prohibited by Romanian authorities from being outside after 2 pm. After Mayor Popovici was sacked, the deportations continued.

It was impossible to go anywhere in the lands where Jews once lived in Ukraine without coming smack up against the Holocaust. In every town and city, in synagogues and cemeteries, the ghosts of the past were in attendance, hovering over the present. I kept coming up against my inability to comprehend the enormity of the horror, to feel the reality of the massive extermination. Each day it grew bigger, more present. Each night, I tried to process what I had learned, without being overwhelmed and swallowed up. My mind heard the facts and listened to the stories. But my heart tried to protect me by pushing my feelings away.

The museum has a wonderful collection of daily objects, and, with much relief, I moved away from the Holocaust displays and stared at artifacts that my grandmother and her family might have used or known in Minkowitz. Although Chernowitz was much larger and more prosperous than the tiny *shtetl* I hailed from, perhaps my ancestors had seen similar forms for making table knives, used the same kind of playing cards, Passover plates, prayer shawls, and *dreydls*—spinning tops the kids played with during Hanukah. Did my grandmother ever see a *chalitsa* shoe, which had always piqued my interest? The *chalitsa* shoe custom goes back to Biblical times and is described in Deuteronomy. If a man's brother died childless, he was obligated to marry the widow, unless the latter released him from his obligation. The intriguing ritual involved the widow taking off the shoe of her brother-in-law and reciting prescribed words, which removed from him the obligation of marrying her. Then she spat on the ground. This was all done in front of witnesses, so it was official. I am not sure if this is still practiced anywhere in the world, and I wondered if any of my ancestors had witnessed a *chalitsa* shoe ceremony in Minkowitz. Throughout the trip, I was always trying to learn details and information, so that I could conjure up images of how my grandmother lived in her *shtetl*. I wanted to be prepared so that when I arrived in Minkowitz, I had a sense of what the life was like in the surrounding area and in the village.

When we left the museum, without asking Alex where we were going next, and before he said a word, I could feel in my bones that we were getting closer and closer to Minkowitz. I experienced an odd mixture of anxiety and anticipation, as though I were advancing toward my destiny.

We stopped in Khotyn, where the population was mostly Jewish before the Holocaust, and visited an old fort where Moldovans, Turks, Poles, and Russians had died in a succession of bloody battles between occupiers and occupied, fighting over who owned and controlled the land.

"On the other side of the fort is Podolya, the region your ancestors came from," Alex announced.

I started to tremble. The feeling in my bones was accurate: we were getting closer. And although I had prepared for this trip all my life, I wasn't ready. That is why I had felt anxious. I wanted to behold

Minkowitz, but something inside of me wasn't ready to go. Maybe it wasn't my destiny, and I would never get to Minkowitz. Perhaps my fate was to know Minkowitz only in my imagination, and the *shtetl* would remain as fictional as Anatevka in *Fiddler on the Roof.* My mind grew frantic, and my thoughts were contradictory and wild.

"*Meir red fin hitz,*" as my grandmother would say. I'm talking with a feverish mind, delirious, making no sense.

I stared through the bars of a fortress window that looked out on Podolya; the bars were an appropriate metaphor for how I felt, that there was a barrier between me and my grandmother's *shtetl*. I had an ominous feeling that some emergency was going to happen that would force me to abort the trip. Something would prevent me from ever getting there. Maybe it wasn't meant to be. Why hadn't I gone before, years ago, when I first learned where Minkowitz was? Why had the time never seemed appropriate? It still didn't feel right. I wasn't ready. There was more I needed to do, some kind of internal preparation. It was as though I were waiting for a sign, a green light, a go-ahead to finally step on my ancestral land.

"Judie," Alex called. "Time to go."

But it wasn't time to go. Not yet. There was still more preparation I had to do. And I was nervous and troubled because I didn't even know what it was.

A Chalista shoe.

A barred view of ancestral lands.

The castle of Kamenetz-Podolsk.

CHAPTER SIXTEEN -- TREMBLING BEFORE THE CASTLE

Because Alex is a scholar and researcher, I never confided in him about the six clues, and how I had carried them in my mind and heart all of my life. I reminded him repeatedly that the most important thing was Minkowitz, and I didn't want to be rushed when we were there.

During our trip, I asked him endless questions about whatever we were seeing at the moment. But I never inquired about where we were going next, never looked at a map, and never referred to the original itinerary. He led, we followed, and all I asked was that he share his knowledge about our surroundings. Paul shot photos, I took copious notes, and Alex flipped through the extensive Rolodex of his mind and provided answers to our queries.

I was as expectant as Marco Polo and Ibn Batuta—a fourteenth century Moroccan Berber adventurer and travel writer— as we drove along a two-lane country road lined with trees, accompanied by the intermittent honking of geese. Churches and houses began to appear; the latter were constructed of stucco and brick, and were separated from the road by metal gates. As we got closer to what was obviously a city, modern buildings made of brick and cement came into view. More cars appeared on the road, people sat at cafes and children played near a fountain in a park. We drove across a high limestone bridge and looked down at a steep canyon, carved by glaciers, with sheer rock walls, trees, a few abodes, and the winding Smotrych River below.

"This bridge was built in the nineteenth century to provide access across the canyon to the Old Town," Alex announced. "Sometimes people bungee jump from here."

On the other side of the bridge was a historic town, bathed in the golden rays of late afternoon sun. The river and gorge extended all the way around it, creating a peninsula, and providing natural defense and fortification.

"What is the name of this town?" I asked Alex.

"Kamenetz-Podolsk," he replied matter-of-factly.

"KAMENETZ-PODOLSK!" I screamed. "It's one of the clues."

"What clues?" Alex asked.

I wasn't comfortable revealing the six clues, so, instead, I presented one of them as fact.

"My grandmother said this was the nearest city to her village. Kamenetz-Podolsk. I can't believe I am here. I am in the land of my grandmother!" And with that I bolted from the car.

Alex smiled indulgently as I walked from one old building to another. Most were yellow or pink, in the Early Russian Classical architectural style prevalent at the beginning of the nineteenth century. They were predominantly simple, two-story houses, with numerous windows and balconies.

"Would these have been here when my grandmother was a child, in the late nineteenth and early twentieth centuries?"

"Yes, for sure," Alex answered.

I walked away from Alex and Paul, wanting to breathe in the air of Kamenetz-Podolsk. Had my grandmother ever been here? Had her father, the *melamed,* the teacher, come here to get official papers that would let the family immigrate to America? Had any of my ancestors placed their feet on these same stones, admired the edifices, looked down at the steep canyon and the river?

"Alex, please," I begged, "tell me what you know."

Apparently, in the year 1900, Kamenetz-Podolsk had a population of almost 35,000 people, half of whom were Jewish, but many had begun immigrating to the United States in the late 1800's.

I so appreciated Alex. He was my connection, my pusher of Eastern European information to which I had become addicted. I had learned on the trip that some Jews had lived prosperous lives, and were integrated into the culture that surrounded them. But I knew that such secular prosperity was far away from Minkowitz, and was convinced that everything within the geographical sphere of the *shtetl* conformed to the mental images I had; they were fashioned from *Fiddler on the Roof* and Roman Vishniac's heart-rending *shtetl* photos of pious, poverty-stricken and ghettoized Jews. Well, it turns out that of course *Fiddler* is a fiction and, so, apparently, were the photos of Vishniac. Although he shot and documented the broad and varied life of Eastern European *shtetl* inhabitants, only the photos that depicted grinding poverty, misery and religious piety were released to engender support and contributions to a Jewish relief organization. Although the purpose may have been noble, the falsification was not. And even though this is now known, the images Roman Vishniac created are seared into the memories of many, many people who saw his photos. If you say "*shtetl*," most people conjure up the images of Vishniac.

In my mind, everyone who lived in the small villages was religious, and bound by tradition. There were no secular or unaffiliated Jews. I imagined that the downside was a lack of religious and cultural diversity, but the upside was that the villagers participated in a rich and cohesive communal life where they banded together in times of joy and periods of oppression. I pictured Minkowitz as a spit of a village, and figured that Kamenetz-Podolsk was, at best, a bigger dot on the map, an obscure town where some administrative tasks were carried out and nothing of note happened. It was a kind of Minkowitz Plus.

In fact, the reality was much more fertile and febrile than my imagination. In the eighteenth century, there was a rift in the Jewish community in Kamenetz-Podolsk, with fierce conflict between two groups: those who followed the rabbinic teachings, oral law and commentaries found in the Talmud, and those who were Frankists, followers of Jacob Frank. The latter claimed to be the reincarnation of the self-proclaimed Messiah, Sabbatai Zevi.

I had heard the unusual story of Sabbatai Zevi long before coming to Ukraine, and I found it dramatic, gripping, and ultimately heartbreaking. In the seventeenth century, during a period when

Bohdan Chmielnicki led a Cossack rebellion against Polish domination and spearheaded massacres of huge swaths of the Jewish population, Sabbatai Zevi arose to offer hope and salvation. He was well-schooled in traditional, rabbinic Judaism, but he was also inspired by Kabbalah and mystical teachings. An ascetic, he was said to fast frequently and even scourge himself. He proclaimed to his many followers—called Sabbateans– that he was the long-awaited Messiah who would herald an era of peace and return his people to the Holy Land. Jews were so miserable, and their ranks so decimated, that they clung to his words, visions, and promises. He preached that in Messianic times the old order and laws didn't need to be followed, and he changed numerous traditional customs and practices. As he got deeper into mysticism, he staged esoteric events, like marrying the *Torah*. An inspired and inspirational leader, Zevi attracted many devoted followers, including some prominent rabbis.

Then, in a stunning reversal, at the age of 40, Zevi converted to Islam—it is unclear if this was by choice or by force—and some of his adherents followed him. Most were shocked and devastated. They felt abandoned and betrayed by the "False Messiah." Yet, even after his conversion and death, many remained loyal to him and his teachings. Even today, when Zevi has been vilified and rejected for many generations, groups like the Donmeh in Turkey are still secret followers. On the surface, they are Islamic; in secret they are Jews who adhere to the precepts of Sabbatai Zevi.

In Kamenetz-Podolsk, in the eighteenth century, there was renewed hope among Sabbateans when Jacob Frank claimed he was

Sabbatai Zevi's reincarnation, and also the reincarnation of Jacob, the grandson of patriarch Abraham, from whose loins the twelve tribes of Israel emerged. Frank said he was the Messiah. He deified himself, had revelations and visions, and espoused new codes of behavior, including the concept of purification through transgression. In other words, by breaking the traditional laws, one would become pure. His followers were reputed to practice polyamory, and it is said there was a lot of wife swapping and swinging going on. It sounded to me like a variant of the sexual liberation of the 1960's, with a Messianic, Eastern European spin.

Frank did not accept Talmudic teachings, but he embraced Kabbalah and accepted the Christian doctrine of the Trinity. Arguably, Frankism was no longer Judaism, but was, instead, a separate religion. In 1757, there was a religious debate, under the aegis of the local Bishop, where the rabbis and Frankists faced off. The Bishop declared that the Frankists were the victors, and he ordered all copies of the Talmud burned publicly. When the Bishop died, the Frankists were persecuted by the rabbis, and Frank eventually converted to Christianity.

All of this transpired in the largest nearby town my grandmother knew of; clearly, it was "the big city" to her. Did she have any idea of the story of Jacob Frank, or Sabbatai Zevi? Was Minkowitz less monolithic and monochromatic than I thought? Were there rifts in Minkowitz when my grandmother lived, or were they all religious, tradition-bound and unquestioning? Why had I never asked my grandmother about these things? How could I get answers? There must have been intellectuals in the village. My great-grandfather was a *melamed*, a teacher, although my mother told me that all he did was train boys for their *bar mitzvahs*. Were there political and religious discussions among the learned men in the synagogue? How can life be so unfair that there is no ancestral tree I can shake to dislodge answers to such questions?

Alex interrupted my internal monologue and told us a little about the history of Kamenetz-Podolsk. It was possibly founded by ancient Dacians, and, in 1241, it was destroyed by Mongol Tatar invasions.

As he spoke, I receded into my own mind again. When I grew up, my mother always teased me that I was *"fargreent"*—green—because I had a sallow complexion. Like many Asian people, I had very little body hair, and was an extremely cheap drunk who was in an altered state after half a glass. I always imagined that one of my ancestors, far back in time, had been raped by a Mongol or other Asian raider, and that I had his blood in my veins. One day, Paul and I hosted a group of monks in our house, and one of them, a Chinese priest, looked at me as he crossed the threshold.

"You are one of us," he said.

That sealed the deal. I had deep Asian ancestry, if not in fact, then at least in my imagination. In the streets of Kamenetz-Podolsk, I learned that there were, indeed, Mongol invasions, with brutal, reckless, rape and pillage. I shuddered to think that back in time, one of the ancestral women in my lineage had been forced at knifepoint or sword point to offer up her body to a rampaging Mongol Tatar. The *fargreent* one had a reason for being *fargreent*, or, more precisely, yellow-tinged. I had been right all along. There was Asian blood flowing in my veins.

I came back from my ponderings to the sound of Alex's voice. He said that Kamenetz-Podolsk had been ruled at different times by Poland, Austria Hungary, Ukraine, and the Soviet Union. It was a multi-ethnic city, although some of those ethnicities had suffered dreadfully. Poles and Ukrainians had been deported to Siberia by the Soviets. And in 1941, over the course of two days, 23,600 Jews were the victims of the first Nazi mass massacre as part of the Final Solution, the elimination and annihilation of Jews.

We walked around the Old Town, past the City Hall with its clock tower, the sixteenth-century Orthodox Cathedral of Saints Peters and Paul, the church of the Holy Trinity, and several Renaissance structures. Alex pointed out a two-story restaurant with 15 windows and a crenelated roof; it had been a synagogue in the seventeenth century. Apparently, Jews had lived around the synagogue, but most of the buildings in that area had been bombed and destroyed in the Second World War.

Then Alex came to a halt, and we beheld in the distance a vision from a fairytale: a sprawling castle and fortress complex with towers, high stone walls and ramparts. As we stood there, the sun set and the multicolored lights of the magnificent fortress came on. It was pure Disney—magical, twinkling, redolent of royalty and romance. Alex said the complex had been built, modified, and expanded from the eleventh to the eighteenth centuries. The Old Town and castle had been nominated as a UNESCO World Heritage site, and Kamenetz-Podolsk was named one of the Seven Wonders of Ukraine.

I strained to listen to his words. All I could think about was:

Had my grandmother been here? Did she know there was a castle? Had she seen the fortress? Had she stood where I was standing? Did she ever leave her village, except to immigrate to the United States? Did her family read newspapers? Did they know what was going on in Kamenetz-Podolsk? And how far was Kamenetz-Podolsk from Minkowitz? I never asked Alex. I just wanted to discover it myself.

That night, we slept at the Hotel Kleopatra, one of the most curious hotels I have ever encountered. The architecture was an impossible, extravagant combination of Greek columns, balconies, and windows adorned with floral motifs executed in plaster. It looked like several eighteenth-century houses had been restored, connected, and transformed into a 4-star hotel. Inside we walked through and past a bowling alley, a billiard room, a spa center with three saunas, an aromatherapy room where the eyes of a Cleopatra mural followed us wherever we walked, a space for playing chess, an artfully-designed swimming pool area adorned with waterfalls and a mosaic of Cleopatra, a separate room sculpted to look like a cave, lounging rooms, a recreation room where little children were celebrating a birthday, a "barrel disco" where the seats were made from old wine barrels, and a hunters' restaurant with deer skins on the chairs. And all these amenities were for only 83 rooms! A large wall near the reception area was covered with a mural of Lithuanian knights who were hunting for deer. The deer brought them to a river, to a land of stones, to what would become Kamenetz-Podolsk.

"Are you Ukrainian?" the woman at the reception desk asked me.

"Sure. In a past life," Alex and Paul told her.

Ordinarily, I would have laughed. But I felt my sense of humor draining away. I realized that the ancestral quest of mine was serious business. It was a deep matter of identity. All my life I had needed to know where I came from. It was not a casual quest. This was the most important trip of my life. Somewhere inside of me I was Ukrainian. Maybe what Alex and Paul said in jest was true. Anything was possible. Maybe I had been here in a past life.

From the ample picture windows on one side of our large, fully-carpeted room, with a king size bed covered with a gold and blue bedspread, pale wood armoire, desk, and an orange-colored, upholstered sofa and hassock, Paul and I had a view of a minaret topped by the Virgin. Once it had been a mosque, and then later it became a church. On the other side of the room, near a pale gold armchair, we had an expansive view of where there used to be a monastery, and we could see the Town Hall. We were in the oldest part of town where I am always happiest when we travel. I want to sink into history, to be surrounded by ancient walls, to understand the past. I look at historic architecture, walk on cobblestone streets, seek clues to the past in music, art, clothes. For me, the past always seems to be calling out: "remember me, remember me." I feel a sense of duty to keep the past alive by observing, listening, learning, writing about the past, so that those who lived before us are not overlooked or forgotten.

We had dinner at Pid Bramoyo restaurant, under the city gate, looking out at the fortress. I wanted to consume everything from

Kamenetz-Podolsk, to get as close as possible to the life my grandmother left behind. I ordered "*Po Domasbniomy*," a stew of pork (I am glad my grandmother will never read these words and know I ate the dreaded, forbidden ingredient), potato, beans, mushrooms, sour cream, and garlic. It was preceded by *borscht* (which my grandmother did eat) with *pampushkas*, which were little buns with garlic sauce. Paul ordered the "Purse of Katherine II"—a combination dish with pork filet (forgive him, Grandma), smoked meat, mushrooms and cheese.

"Do you think it's wrong to eat pork here, in the land of our ancestors?" I asked Paul.

He quoted a rabbi friend of ours who maintains that God cares about what comes out of your mouth, not what goes into it.

With that, I ate the delicious meal with relish. The perfectly prepared *borscht* was accompanied by white beans laced with garlic. We were served new wine, which was poured from a barrel, and ordered Russian cheese for dessert. We didn't talk much, listening to the frogs around us in the darkness, singing their mating song. When we left the restaurant, we paused to look at the statue of a Cossack leader who massacred the Turks during the holy holiday of Ramadan.

I had always joked about my grandmother thinking Kamenetz-Podolsk was the big city. I was sure it was a corner of Nowhere, a little Nothing. But it was lovely, deep, meaningful, with a layer of natural beauty and, below that, layers of great tragedy and sadness.

Back in our hotel room, we got ready for bed and turned out the lights. As we lay there in the darkness, Paul's last words before he fell asleep were, "Alex said we are very close to Minkowitz now. Tomorrow we will be there."

I started to tremble. I couldn't understand why. Instead of being excited, I was once again apprehensive, confused, fearful. All my life I had wanted to be here. Now I was here. I was afraid of what I would find, and what I wouldn't find in Minkowitz. Perhaps the trip would be aborted by a call from the United States, informing me that I had to come home at once. Or Paul or I would suddenly fall sick. I tried to stop my brain from fabricating scenarios of doom. I flipped over and over in bed, trying to fall asleep, attempting to quiet my mind. I tried deep breathing, meditation, flexing and relaxing my muscles. I realized that I was trembling because being in the land of my grandmother was shaking me to the marrow of my bones. It was the most important trip I had taken in my life.

"I'm almost there, Gram," I intoned quietly, and then, finally, I fell asleep.

Art at the Kleopatra Hotel depicts the founding of the city.

View of Kamenetz Podolsk from the castle.

The entrance to the hellish silica mine.

CHAPTER SEVENTEEN -- THE MINE

In the morning, Paul cheerfully announced that it was Minkowitz day. I didn't respond. He bolted down breakfast so we could hit the road. I ate in a desultory fashion, pushing my eggs listlessly around my plate.

"Ready?" Alex said as he bounded over to our table.

"I'd like to see more of Kamenetz Podolsk," I informed him. "I am sure there are churches we should visit, statuary we should see, old cobblestone streets we need to explore. Of course we want to visit the castle. We don't want to miss that."

Alex and Paul exchanged quizzical looks, and then Alex began a tour, just as I had requested.

"Judie," Paul whispered, "what is going on?"

"Nothing. We're interested in seeing everything, right? Well, we need to explore more of the city."

"But I don't understand. You've talked about this since I've known you. Now we're here. Don't you want to go to Minkowitz?"

As we wandered through the churches and the streets, Paul sidled up to me. "Okay. I think I understand. You're not ready. It's not time to go yet. Is that right?"

I nodded vigorously. I didn't understand myself what was

happening, but Paul's explanation sounded correct.

We visited the castle, walking along the ramparts, and suddenly I stood still, as though listening to a summons from far off. I turned to Paul.

"It's time."

We immediately got into the van and headed towards Minkowitz. I was holding my breath.

"Judie . . .?" Paul said with a look of concern.

I was probably turning blue from not breathing so I smiled slightly, to show him I was okay.

He reached for my hand. I wanted to thank him, but I couldn't speak. I was beyond words, in a realm where memory, longing, fear, anticipation, emotion, and intellect intersect. I gripped his hand and stared out the window of the moving van.

We passed road signs that bore the names of *shtetl*s: Smotrich. Dunaivtsi. This was not a film or a blockbuster Broadway show called *Fiddler on the Roof*. It was reality. "This is real. This is real. I am here. In Ukraine. These are *shtetl*s. This was the land of my grandmother," I said to myself. I had dreamed about it for so long that I had to remind myself that I was in the real place. I had to pay rapt attention to each detail, to remember it before it receded and I could no longer tell the difference between dream and memory. I needed to be more alert and present than I had ever been in my life. I knew in my bones that if I wanted to be connected through time to where I came from, and the people and places that inhabited that world, I had to be fully, deeply, focused and emotionally available to whatever I saw, heard, and felt.

Suddenly I could hear my grandmother's voice speaking to me. It was as clear as though she were a few feet away. *"Gott zu danken.* Thank God. *Mammaleh, Gott zu Danken."* I was on the brink of crying. Paul moved his hand onto my knee and squeezed, letting me know that he was right there, supporting me.

"The name Dunaivtsi comes from Danube," Alex said. "The *shtetl* was largely destroyed in World War II." In the distance I could see modern, nondescript stores, concrete block houses, brick apartment buildings. I tried to prepare myself for the eventuality that Minkowitz would look like this too. I prayed it wouldn't be so, but I feared it would. "Just stay present. Don't project into the future. Be here. Be here. Just observe. Just feel," I told myself.

We continued along the road. Some houses were decorated with woodwork that was carved and painted so that it looked like embroidery. We passed a few older, poorer, wooden houses. Then Vitaly made a right turn on the road that led from Dunaivtsi to Minkowitz. This was the home stretch. I could no longer think clearly. I was in a highly charged and emotional state, fighting back tears as we headed to the *shtetl* that had haunted and called to me all my life.

The houses disappeared. All I saw through the window were endless stretches of green grass, fields, and trees. I heard Alex speaking to Vitaly in Ukrainian, and the van made another right turn. Two women in black *babushkas* that covered their hair and were tied under their chins, watched us pass. Then the car came to a halt. Alex slid out of the front seat and beckoned for us to follow him. He climbed up an embankment and entered the woods along a cement path. Ordinarily, I might have asked him why we were taking a detour on the most auspicious stretch of road of our trip, but I didn't. Too full of feeling to speak, I put one foot ahead of the other and walked after him. Paul was right behind me.

I could hear birds chirping in the trees as we walked. We came to a cement wall that had been tagged with graffiti. And next to it was a white building with a black metal door and a white Jewish star. I wondered what a Jewish symbol was doing in the middle of the forest.

"This was the entry to an old silica mine," Alex said in his matter-of-fact way. "The Germans moved 3,000 Jews from the *shtetl*s here in 1942. The Nazis were drinking vodka as they shot them all, and threw the bodies of the wounded and the dead into the depths of the mineshaft. For the next week, local people said they heard screams of people dying in the bottom of the mine."

In the core of my being, I felt the reaction of the local inhabitants. The echoes of the screams carried into their houses and were with them while they worked, and ate, and slept. It was with them when they woke up, walked, nursed their children, did their wash, hung up their clothes to dry, made love under the covers at night. It rattled them when they cleaned their houses, fed their dogs, repaired the broken leg of a chair, cleaned crumbs off the table. It took a week for all the people in the mine to die. Then the absence of sound was as unsettling as the screams had been. The air reeked of death. It settled in the trees and vegetable gardens, wrapped around the woodpiles, permeated the curtains and the fluffy comforters in the babies' cribs.

At that moment, all the unreality of the Holocaust dissolved inside of me. I had spoken to survivors, visited camps, read countless books, gone to museums, seen films. Nothing had ever penetrated the numbness until I stood in the forest at the entrance to this mine. I was literally knocked off balance by the realization that this would have been my family's fate. I grabbed Paul's arm, trying to steady myself. If my grandmother had not come to the United States, I would not have been born. My mother would not exist. There would be no person I knew as myself. I would never have gone to school, made friends, played stickball, eaten *kugel*, shopped for clothes, fought with my mother, mourned my father, waited for the phone to ring, stayed up all night writing, met Paul, fallen in love, laughed until I gasped, cried until my eyes swelled and I could hardly see. I owed my life, and every experience I had ever had, to my ancestors who had left behind the world I was traveling through, to bravely board a ship and sail in steerage class to face the unknown in America.

I could see the twisted limbs in the deep, dark bottom of the mine. I gagged from the horror of the living lying helplessly alongside the dead bodies of their beloveds, their children, and their neighbors. I could smell blood and urine and feces. I could hear their screams alternating with their prayers, and their calling out to God, begging for mercy, for help, for an explanation of why this was happening. I could crawl inside their minds and see them reliving their short lives. I could feel their longing to live and their wanting to die, to end the torment. I could hear them begging the Nazis for mercy, even as I saw that the woods were empty and the Nazis were long gone. Every fiber in me ached with the knowledge and the pain of what those agonized souls had endured. A week. Seven days. There was no Sabbath that week. Their only Sabbath was a release from suffering into death. They could have been my people. My grandmother and great-grandmother, my uncles, aunts, and cousins. Writhing to their deaths at the bottom of a mine in a forest. And then, silence.

I looked again at the entrance to the mine. Now it seemed uncannily like the entryway to a mausoleum. I knew we were standing on a cemetery of corpses, bones piled high at the bottom of the mineshaft. I looked at Paul, who was pale and expressionless. I knew that he, too, knew.

I noticed two niches in the cement wall where people had left candles and stones. I picked up a stone from the ground and placed it there. Paul placed one too. "Rest in peace," I intoned. "After all your suffering in body and soul, rest in peace."

As we walked back to the van without speaking, I could hear the birdsongs again. They had a lugubrious undertone, a deep woe underneath the buoyant chirp of life. The path we were walking on was the path the Jews had walked to their execution. Did they know? Did they suspect that one minute they would be standing on the earth, and the next minute they would lie under it, alive or dead, shot through the head and the heart?

As we neared the van, we met a woman, a man, and a little girl who carried pails, happily collecting mushrooms. We said hello, and I begged Alex to ask them if they knew what had happened in the forest at the mine. As soon as he posed the question, the woman and the man looked down and grew sad. They said that everyone in Dunaivtsi knew about it. The elders remembered those screams. The dead were still ghosts that haunted Dunaivtsi, their voices echoing in the ears of the living.

"Did your family talk to you about it?"

"No."

"So how did you know?"

"We knew. We all just knew."

"Have you told your daughter?"

We all turned to look at her. She was swinging her pail of mushrooms.

"No," the parents said. And they continued shaking their heads no as they walked off into the woods to hunt for mushrooms, turning back briefly towards us to wave goodbye.

"Judie …" Paul said, "The next stop is Minkowitz. Are you…?"

"Yes, I am. The past and the present are aligned for me now. I am ready."

Alex got into the car. Paul got into the car. I took a deep breath and climbed in last. Vitaly turned on the engine.

At long last, the time had come.

Minkowitz after 102 years.

CHAPTER EIGHTEEN -- MINKOWITZ AT LAST

As we drove towards Minkowitz, I thought about my grandmother, sailing in steerage on the *President Lincoln* to Ellis Island in 1910. I wondered what she was feeling as the ship approached the New York harbor—fear, excitement, anticipation, confusion.

I realized that I felt similar emotions. Fear that my grandmother's Minkowitz was no more, and that I was in for a colossal disappointment. I had waited all my life and traveled such a long distance to encounter Soviet-style apartment buildings with tiny balconies that served as drying racks for nondescript, factory-made, modern clothes. I felt excitement at the prospect of seeing my ancestral village, confusion because all the feelings wrapped around each other and I couldn't sort them out. I also felt foolish. Why was I so obsessed with a tiny corner of the world? Maybe my mother and sisters were right to sweep it away into the dust pile of useless memories. And finally, I felt foolish because I had waited until mid-afternoon for the visit, and I knew we would only have a few hours there before we had to drive to a hotel. Why hadn't I gone there first thing in the morning?

I went over the six facts that I had clung to since childhood.

Tuesday market. She dried tobacco leaves. She lived at the bottom of a hill. The Russian girls went to school on top of the hill. The floor of the house was made of goat dung. Kamenetz Podolsk. At least I had been to Kamenetz Podolsk.

We passed by modest, cement houses, a few locals selling mushrooms, and vast, open fields.

"Beans," I said to Paul.

"What?"

"Look. In the field, they're growing beans. My grandmother said she ate beans. At least it's some validation of what she told me."

"Goat," I proclaimed about ten minutes later.

"Yes. . ."

"If there's a goat today, there probably were goats 102 years ago. And if there were goats, there was goat shit. And if there was goat shit, maybe it's true that . . ."

My voice trailed off. I wanted to see the Minkowitz of my imagination. I was desperate. I couldn't bear the thought that everything I heard from my grandmother was gone, maybe untrue. My mother had said that what my grandmother told me was a fiction. That there were no tobacco fields, and the girls weren't allowed to work. That the floors were made of dirt, not goat dung. That the *shtetl* probably no longer existed

"Look, Judie, look," said Paul, excitedly pointing to a large, white sign on the side of the road, which announced the name of the village in Ukrainian: Minkivtsi. The car was still moving but I jumped out, dashing through a small field of poppies, encircling the sign with my arms, hugging it as though it were a long-lost friend.

"Minkivtsi, Minkivtsi," I intoned. "Paul, we're here. This is it."

I began to cry. Tears poured down my face and dribbled from my chin. Alex and Vitaly looked at me quizzically.

"Is something wrong?" Alex asked, concerned.

I couldn't speak. A cow, grazing on a hill behind the sign, mooed. She probably wasn't used to visitors.

I clung to the sign, wanting to hold onto every minute. By nightfall, this would all be a memory. Finally, I let go and got back into the car, imploring Vitaly to drive as slowly as he possibly could, so I could imprint everything.

We drove past cornfields. "*Kornbluth*"—corn flower blooms. That was my grandmother's maiden name. She was named for the corn that grew around the *shtetl*. What she told me about eating corn was true. Or did "*bluth*" come from German and mean blood? She married Isidor Kriegsfeld—Isidor Battlefield. Did their two names connote blood and war and battlefields? That would have been appropriate. My mother had a tumultuous relationship with her father. I had a tumultuous relationship with my mother. Blood or blooms? Blooms or blood?

We passed a sausage factory. This was the main street of Minkowitz, a country road, maybe not very different from the street that ran through Minkowitz in my grandmother's time. I wondered how often she stood at the side of the road, watching an occasional horse-drawn cart go by. Then I saw a well for drawing water with a bucket and a winch in front of an old, abandoned, white building.

"Paul, I need you to take a picture of the well, and that building."

"Why? It's totally uninspiring. You'll never use the photo." Paul responded like the photographer he is.

"Please, I'm begging you. Just do it."

"The building looks interesting," Alex said. "Let's go take a look."

We walked past the well and examined the front and side of the building. The windows were broken, the stucco was cracked and fading. I noticed that Alex had crossed over to a large, administrative-looking building next to it, and was talking animatedly to a pleasantly plump woman in a lavender shirt with ruffled sleeves and a white skirt. He motioned for me to join him, and introduced me to the woman, Natalia Olijnyk, the mayor of Minkowitz.

"I am from Minkowitz," I blurted out.

"I know," she said, and we hugged each other. I started to cry again, and I couldn't stop.

"Don't worry," Alex whispered to me. "You are safe here. No one will hurt you."

He didn't understand why I was crying, and probably imagined I was afraid of anti-Semitism or some other hostile reaction in Minkowitz. How could I explain that I was crying because my soul was trembling, that I was overcome with emotion?

"I will help you any way I can," the Mayor said, as she motioned us to follow her into the building. Just before she entered, she turned to me and said, "It's very curious. If you had come one minute earlier, I would have been inside, in my office, and you wouldn't have found me. If you had come one minute later, I would have been gone, en route home for lunch. The timing is remarkable."

I blinked with incredulity. Was that was why I couldn't leave Kamenetz Podolsk earlier? Was that why Alex stopped at the mine in the forest? Why the men in the van drove up to help me in Boorshtein, the Rabbi appeared at the tomb of the Baal Shem Tov, the Gypsy Baron agreed to talk to us and the Mayor materialized at the moment we needed her? This trip was my destiny. I was fated to go to Minkowitz from the time I was a child. All the elements aligned for me— the people, the places, the timing. It made perfect sense.

"You know," the Mayor told us, "a delegation came here last year to investigate the Holocaust. They were commemorating 70 years since the murder of the Jews and they gave me a little commemorative sculpture from Jerusalem. There were about 40 children among them. They came from Israel, America, and Ukraine. And there's something else. A Jew from Minkowitz named Leysgood has rebuilt his family house here, and even though he lives in Israel, he brings people to see it." I felt an immediate kinship with the man named Leysgood. Even though his family had undoubtedly suffered terribly in Minkowitz in the past, somehow the *shtetl* drew him back and had an emotional hold on him in the present.

The mayor invited us into her office, and called out to her assistant. Together they perused the large archival ledger book that listed family names. In the 1970's, they found the name Kornblatt, with a slightly different spelling. Moses Ben Zionovitch Kornblitt. Born 1919. Worked as a person in charge of storage. He was still in Minkowitz in 1976. How did he survive the mass executions of the Nazis? Did he serve in the Soviet army? What happened to him? Alas, the ledger provided names and dates, but no answers.

"In Soviet times, the Jews and the Ukrainians were very friendly," the Mayor said. "Ukrainians say that Jews are people who know how to live well. They drink less. They organize their households better."

Did Ukrainian people hide and protect Moses Kornblitt? Was he related to me? I started to sob. My mother said that none of my Kornbluths remained behind in Minkowitz. But could this man have been an ancestor?

I couldn't believe I had so many tears. No matter how often I mopped my eyes, they just kept flowing. Then I ceased trying to stop them. I allowed myself to feel. It was a relief to permit my lifelong emotions about Minkowitz to come pouring out.

"Please, can you look up my husband's last name? He is Ross now, but in the Old Country it was Rosen."

The Mayor and her assistant looked through the book. There were no Rosens listed. There were Rossners, and often names had different variants and spellings but were part of the same family.

Paul bent over the ledger book, trying desperately to find a Rosen.

"Rossner could be a different spelling of my name," he said. "Or else... maybe my father and his parents were here for a while and then traveled to another *shtetl*. There was a lot of movement. Maybe they're not listed because they weren't born here. There are a lot of possibilities."

There were tears in Paul's eyes now. He bit his lips, trying to hold them back. I ached for Paul. When he grew up, his mother, who made ice seem warm, disdained his paternal grandparents, and kept him from seeing them. She was descended from German-speaking Jews, and she often said that she had "married beneath her station." She scorned her husband's poor, uneducated, unworldly, Yiddish-speaking parents from the *shtetl*s. She unfairly prevented Paul from knowing his paternal grandparents and experiencing the comforting warmth of their home. He hadn't watched his grandma make chicken soup and *kugel* or drop circles of dough into boiling water to make bagels. Instead, he had eaten the bitter bread and cold imperiousness of his mother's family. I wished I could share my grandmother with him so that he, too, could have a grandma Tick Tock who protected him from the evil eye and brought a gentle presence into his life.

"Paul, do you think your ancestors came from Minkowitz?" I asked him.

"Yes."

"If you think you came from here, you most likely did. It doesn't matter if you can't find the exact name in the ledger book. We're from Minkowitz. It's our *shtetl*." This time I squeezed his hand for reassurance, as he had done for me so many times before.

He nodded vigorously. We both wanted to believe that Paul had been a raisin sorter and a chicken plucker in Minkowitz. We wanted to believe that the spoon his father gave us, which he said came from Minkowitz, and was used for our wedding, was proof that the Rosens and the Kornbluths both came from this *shtetl*. We share a life, and we share a heritage.

"What is the building next door? The one with the well," I blubbered at the mayor.

"A tobacco plant. It's closed now, but the women and girls used to sit out back, drying tobacco leaves, hanging them on ropes."

Tobacco leaves! Just what my grandmother told me. It was true. It was one of the facts I had held onto for so many years, and here I was, staring at the place where my grandmother worked as a 10-year-old girl.

"Was there a school here, where Russian girls studied and wore uniforms?"

"Let me show you," she offered. Close to the mayor's office was an old, two-story school building. There were tasteful designs embedded in the limestone facing, and large windows lined the front and sides; 14 on the side and 18 across the front. The stones, apparently, had been recycled from an old Catholic church. They were perfectly hewn, and almost no mortar was needed in the construction.

"When was the school built?" I asked the mayor.

"It is built in the classical Czarist style," Alex said. The Mayor agreed. "The Czarist period, when your grandmother lived here," she added. But was it the school my grandmother recalled throughout her life and into old age?

The Mayor of Minkowitz.

The mayor got into our van, and we drove down a hill, where she pointed out all the houses on the right side of the river Ushitsa that once belonged to Jews. They were made of small wooden boards, covered with mud and then stuccoed over. Some of them were inhabited and others were abandoned. We were at the bottom of a hill. Just as my grandmother had described. I got out of the car, stood on the dirt road among the houses, and looked up to the top of the hill. There was the school that we had just seen. The school my grandmother looked at with envy when she was a poor Jewish girl and the Russian schoolgirls wore starched uniforms.

Pools of tears soaked my shirt. It was true. My grandmother gave me the most precious gift when I was little: information about her *shtetl*. I carried it with me all my life. And now I was seeing it, exactly the way she described it to me. I could feel her envy, her desire to go to that school, to learn grammar, history, math, and Russian. To rise above the restrictions placed on the lives of Jews, and be free, just like the Russian girls. I was so sorry my grandmother never had that opportunity. Standing at the bottom of the hill, I understood more of who she was, and what she longed for when she was a young girl. I pictured her in a plain dress, her hair matted by a babushka, looking up at the Russian girls in their starched uniforms, giggling, playing, whispering secrets to each other. She was an outsider, a Jew, an observer of the life she wished she could lead. She went back home to help her mother with chores, while the Russian girls returned to classes after recess. She lived in an atmosphere of fear and tension, as news of pogroms and massacres of Jews reached

Minkowitz. The Russian girls were insouciant, living carefree lives. My grandmother's parents skimped and saved and plotted their relocation to America. The Russian girls would grow up, marry, and have children in the land where they were born.

The Mayor took us to a white plaster house that was owned by Moses Kornblitt's family. In the small front yard, a single cornstalk grew. I backed up when a neighbor opened the door, motioned for us to enter, and I beheld piles of furniture, boxes, and dust everywhere. I was afraid that rats and mice would crawl out from their hiding places and run towards us. No one lived in the house; it was used for storage. When we stepped outside, I wondered about the cornstalk, and who planted it in front of an unoccupied house.

"No one planted that corn," the mayor said. "It is mystical. How did that one cornstalk get here, in front of a house owned by people named Kornblitt, with corn in their name?"

We stopped briefly at the Mayor's office so that I could use the bathroom; I was surprised when she said it was outside. I walked behind the building and saw a wooden hut. Inside were a few worn, weathered slabs of wood with an irregularly shaped hole between them. Next to it were an almost-empty roll of toilet paper and a few pages torn from the local newspaper. The Mayor's official bathroom was probably no different from the outhouse my grandmother and her family used. Minkowitz had a thin veneer of modernity, but underneath were hand-drawn wells, dilapidated outhouses, and re-stuccoed houses that had been inhabited for more than 100 years.

The Mayor offered to introduce us to Nina Simionovna, a

woman in her late 80's, one of the oldest inhabitants in the area, who might remember something. We went to her house. Nina had trouble walking, but, leaning on a walker, she beckoned me to sit next to her outside of her abode. I told her why I was in Minkowitz, and that my grandmother, Esther Kornbluth (or Kornblatt) had left the *shtetl* 102 years ago.

"Kornblatt?" Nina mused. "I knew a Kornblatt. Abraham Kornblatt. When the Nazis came after the Jews, he ran away to a nearby village to get baptized, and he changed his name to Piotr. I tried my best to help him, and not one person in the village ever betrayed him. His whole family was killed, and he, himself, died after the war of natural causes."

Nina Simionovna, keeper of the memories of Minkowitz.

Abraham Kornblatt. Was he a relative? Was he part of the family of Moses Kornblitt? Before coming to Ukraine, I had googled the name Kornbluth, and every variation of the name I could think of, until my hands grew weary on my keyboard. I contacted dozens of people through social media, asking them if their ancestors, or they, themselves, came from Minkowitz. Most never replied or, if they did, they said they had no idea where their family came from, or they would try to find an older relative to ask. I drew a Kornblank until I arrived in Minkowitz. Now, in the course of an hour or two, I learned about Moses and Abraham, although there was no way to ascertain if we had a family link.

"I had a dear Jewish friend named Entsa," Nina reminisced. "One day, I heard Entsa calling my name, 'Nina, Nina.' I will never forget the way she called out to me. I saw her being hit by a Nazi with the butt of his gun. When I ran towards her, the Nazi looked me menacingly and said, 'Do you want to go with her?' Entsa and I cried and cried. The Nazis took her away."

She stopped for a moment. Her eyes had a sad, vacant look, as though she were reliving the moment when Entsa disappeared with the Nazi. Then Nina looked towards a hill in the distance, where there was a stand of several trees.

"They moved the Jews up to that hill and forced them to undress. There were four gendarmes and several Ukrainian shoots-men (police). My family heard shots coming from the hill. One day the shots lasted from morning to night. The Nazis rolled up their sleeves and sang songs while they murdered the Jews. Children were killed with the butts of guns and thrown into the canyon. These people were innocent. They were nice people. They would never betray others. I lost all of my classmates, children we went to school with. My friends and the friends of my sister and brother. From that time, I am the only one of my old friends who is alive today."

It was very painful to sit next to Nina, looking up at the hill where such horrible crimes were committed, imagining the little children, who were alive and vibrant one moment and corpses the next.

"When the shooting stopped, my father took me up to the hill. The earth was moving up and down, up and down, because some of them were still alive, still breathing. It was their final destination. Later, my father planted the tall trees on the site of the communal grave to honor and remember those who were killed."

"Did any Jews survive?" I asked.

"Some were hiding. The Nazis found them and assembled them. They led them to another place and shot them. During the time when the Jews were executed, one of them, a friend of my father's, ran away and came to our house. He lived in the woods and we brought him food. Eventually, he left the woods and was killed. We also were able to rescue one Jewish woman who lived with us during the war. Her name was Luba Mark. I told people that Luba was my sister, and that she had been living in Moldova."

I listened to Nina, and knew that I was in the presence of one of the righteous among the nations. Everything about her was simple and straightforward, without any artifice or guise. I imagined that she came from a poor family, and yet, they had helped their Jewish neighbors and friends at their own peril.

Many years ago, when I lived in Switzerland, I had gone to the home of Anne Frank's father Otto, who lived in Basel. One of the most significant things he told me was that after the war, after his entire family had been wiped out by the Nazis, he went to Germany to find good Germans. He felt that it was important for him, as a human, to look to the good part of human nature, even in the most devastating circumstances. I know that even though many Ukrainians had collaborated in the annihilation of Jews, there were also many good Ukrainians, and I was with one.

"When I was a child, we didn't have enough food," Nina said. "We went through the garbage from the richer folks to get food. I remember that when I came home from school, I stopped at the house of a Jewish friend's family and they sometimes gave me food. Other times, we gave them food. During Passover they gave me *matza*, and we gave them Easter cakes. They made round *matza*; it was very thin and had holes. The Jews and Ukrainians were like one family."

She turned again to look towards the hill, and I reached out and took her hand. I could see her eyes floating back to the past and feel the pain of her loss of Entsa and her other friends. We sat together in silence.

"Nina," I hope we have not tired you too much," I said.

"It's all right. You have come to find out the story of the Jews here, and the story of the village your grandmother left behind. It is important that you know."

An old well and the abandoned tobacco factory.

"If my grandmother hadn't left in 1910, she could have ended up on that hill. I know that."

Nina nodded. I could see that she really was tired.

"Nina," I ventured, "I hope it's okay if I ask you one more question."

She nodded again.

"Do you remember what the floors of the house were made of when you grew up?"

"Yes," she said smiling. "Animal manure."

Goat shit! Somewhere, in a land beyond life, my grandmother was nodding too. The floors of the house were, indeed, made of goat dung. I was so grateful for the confirmation that I reached over and hugged Nina. We held onto each other for a long moment before Paul, Alex and I left. I called out to Nina: "*L'chaim.*" In Hebrew it means "To Life." I wondered if she had any idea how important our meeting was to me. Thanks to her, I learned what happened to the people who stayed behind when my ancestors left. Thanks to her, I had verified the fifth of six facts that linked me to Minkowitz.

It was late in the day and Alex asked what Paul and I wanted to do with the remaining time.

Paul and I decided. We wanted to walk down the dirt streets of Minkowitz. Alex waited in the van, as I stopped in front of houses that had once been occupied by Jews. I tried to imagine mothers making *schmaltz* and children chasing each other, laughing inside the houses. I pictured my mother's grandmother shaping melted wax into balls and getting visions that helped people to heal from what plagued them. I communicated with locals by using hand signs and tossing in a few words in Russian, German, French, English, Yiddish, anything I thought they might understand. I tried to tell them that I came from Minkowitz, that it was my ancestral home. I pointed to the hill where the Jews had been shot. I spoke my grandmother's maiden name. I hoped that, somehow, they understood me.

"Now I'd like to go to the cemetery, Alex," I said. I thought about the photos of tombstones Andrew had sent me 20 years ago. We climbed up a hill, and walked through brush and forest to reach what remained of the Jewish cemetery. An elderly man appeared to act as our guide, and he explained that Jewish people paid him to be the caretaker. I read the inscriptions on stones and looked at dates; they were too recent to have come from the time of my grandmother. We asked him if there were older stones. He said it was too difficult to reach them, but we insisted. So we pushed ahead, up a steep, dirt path that passed through brambles and trees until we reached a few, isolated, older headstones. Still, they did not come from the time my family was in Minkowitz. The man pointed to a spot where he said there used to be a Jewish house. Some gold was found there, buried where the Jewish people had left it. The people who found it thought that the gold would bring them luck, but it didn't. In fact, they had bad luck afterwards. We tried to penetrate deeper into the brambles and forest to find older tombs, but our arms and legs were getting scratched and we decided to turn back. I still had the photos Andrew sent me two decades ago. He had preserved the memories of the tombstones that were now swallowed up. History was disappearing so quickly, fading during my lifetime. Who would know about the tombstones in fifty years?

It was blazing hot, and we stopped for a drink at the only convenience store/café we saw in town. I announced to everyone within earshot that I came from Minkowitz, and was returning 102 years after my grandmother left.

Off to the side, two bearlike Russian men sat at a table drinking. They waved us over, repeated aloud that my roots were in Minkowitz and welcomed me effusively to my ancestral town. Then they began to hug me and kiss me, pouring cognac for Paul, Alex, and me. Bottoms up. To my grandmother's family in Minkowitz. Then they poured again, and we toasted to Paul's ancestors from Minkowitz. Paul closed his eyes, taking in the moment when he, too, could recognize and acknowledge those who came before him. When he opened his eyes, I saw a few tears, for the second time that day.

The Russians were already several sheets to the wind, and they got louder and friendlier and soon we were laughing and munching pickles and chocolate and they were telling me how Ukrainian I looked, and how wonderful it was for me to come back after 102 years.

"What is that large field across from where we are sitting?" I asked.

"It's where the Jewish market was," they replied. "It still takes place on the same day. Tuesday."

I stifled my sobs. The school my grandmother had looked up at. The place where her family lived at the bottom of the hill. Goat dung for floors. A tobacco plant where women and children dried leaves. And now, the marketplace where they bought beans and corn and beets.

"*Gott zu danken, mamaleh*," I heard my grandmother say. "You have come here. You have witnessed my life."

My mother was wrong. My grandmother was right. She had left me with the treasure of six facts. All of them were still there, as though waiting to be seen, waiting to have their existence affirmed. I stood there, looking back at Minkowitz before we departed.

I sent out silent blessings to all the Jews who had lived and died in Minkowitz. To those who had been shot. To those who had escaped. To the righteous of Minkowitz who had helped to save Jews. To the people of Minkivtsi, who had been so open with us, and invited us to come back. To the mayor. To Nina. To the man who had led us to the tombstones. To Paul's ancestors. To my grandmother, whose six facts were a roadmap that led me to this moment.

A hundred and two years had passed. I was home.

Paul toasts his ancestors with one of the Russian men.

Jenny Spektor and the artwork in a thriving Jewish Community Center, Odessa.

The next generation.

CHAPTER NINETEEN -- SAYING GOOD-BYE

I was afraid that after my tear-soaked visit to Minkowitz, anything else would be anti-climactic. We would have flown home directly from Minkowitz, but it was unlikely that a village with ramshackle outhouses and wells with buckets and winches would have an international airport. Fortunately, we came up with a solution.

One of the few things my mother told me about my grandmother was that she left Minkowitz and sailed to New York from Odessa, which is why we decided to leave from Odessa, as my grandmother had done.

It turns out that my mother's information about my grandmother's port of departure was guesswork, and not fact. According to the Ellis Island archives—which I found right before we left on our trip—Esther Kornbluth, from Meinkowice, Russia, sailed on the *President Lincoln* from Hamburg, Germany at the tender age of 17 and arrived in New York on December 28, 1910. She had a fair complexion, as I do, and measured five feet four inches, which is four inches taller than I am. She had black hair and blue eyes; mine are green. Her passage was paid by her father, Jossel Kornbluth, who, according to my mother, took my grandmother and her sisters to America and later paid for his wife, son, and daughter-in-law to come.

So there I was in Odessa, on the Black Sea, under a merciless sun, with a non-refundable return flight booked and paid for, even though it wasn't my grandmother's city of departure. According to Alex, people from the *shtetl*s rarely sailed from Odessa to the United States. Russia did not have many transatlantic crossings, and it was cheaper and shorter to sail from Bremen, Antwerp, or Hamburg, as my grandmother did.

I was terribly disappointed, and didn't care if I lay like a piece of *matza* all day in our air-conditioned hotel room.

"There's a lot to see here," Alex said. "Before the war, it had the third largest Jewish population in the world, after New York and Warsaw."

I shrugged.

"This was part of our grandparents' universe, even if they didn't sail from here," Paul chimed in.

I shrugged again, listlessly following Alex's index finger as it pointed to a memorial to the victims of the pogrom of 1905 in Odessa. "That may be why your ancestors fled from Minkowitz," he said.

The words "Minkowitz" and "ancestors" were like a vitalizing infusion, and in an instant all my energy came back. It wasn't simply more information related to the *shtetl* that woke me up. It was the lure of deeper connection to those who came before me, and the resuscitation of the life they left behind when they stepped off the boat in Ellis Island. They didn't want to talk about it because their memories were dappled with so much poverty and pain. But, for me, learning about that pain was necessary so that I could honor them for their courage, forbearance, and endurance.

"There were pogroms against the Jews before 1905," Alex said. "They began in the first quarter of the nineteenth century." He explained that the earlier mob attacks might have been the result of rival ethnicities, rather than strictly anti-Semitic outpourings. But the horrors of 1905 definitely fall into the latter category.

I entered a mental Time Machine, as I do on my Mac computer, rapidly flashing backwards through earlier dates and earlier times. I knew I had heard something about Odessa and a pogrom when I was a child, but I couldn't find the person who had mentioned it. Was it my grandmother? An aunt or uncle? Had I read it?

According to Alex, the 1905 pogrom happened during a period of social unrest throughout the country, and especially in Odessa. The Russian government had lost the war in Japan. Corruption was rampant. The mutiny of the crew of the battleship Potemkin—which sailed into Odessa on the night of the rebellion— fanned the flames of anti-government sentiment in the city. The government tried to control the unrest, and they unleashed reactionary forces. Rampaging gangs of young people, which may have included some undercover cops, stripped and beat anyone who looked Jewish. Estimates of the number of Jews and non-Jews killed ranges from a few hundred to several thousand. There were countless injuries, and homes, apartments and shops were violently attacked and damaged.

The echoes of this pogrom spread to the *shtetl*s, and I think 1905 was the straw that broke the *shtetl*s' backs; it was clearly time to get out of Dodgeowitz before things got worse. When my grandmother and her father and sisters set sail in 1910, I believe it was a response to the terror they felt from the 1905 pogrom and the rising tide of anti-Semitism.

Maybe there was a reason we were in Odessa, and it wasn't an accident. Maybe the story of my grandmother, her *shtetl*, and the world she came from had one last chapter that was being revealed to me at the end of my voyage, on the shores of the Black Sea.

Alex pointed out a cemetery where Gypsies and Jews are buried. Before the trip, this would have been an odd detail. Now it conjured up images of the Gypsy Baron and the Jews of Moldova. I realized that my whole way of seeing my grandmother's world had deepened and changed. It was no longer a stereotypical mental image framed in six facts. It was complex, and I had concrete pictures in my mind that I can draw on for the rest of my life.

Alex showed us every Jewish site he could think of—the poor section of Moldovanka, where Jews used to live; the small, cement building where the first Zionist meeting and the first meetings of the Jewish Enlightenment in Odessa were held. Then he led us inside the Moorish-style, two-story, Migdal Jewish Community Center, by far the most hopeful, vibrant place we visited in Ukraine. According to Jenny Spektor, the smart, spunky assistant to the director, the center has more than 100 programs that are offered to everyone in the community, from tots to nonagenarians. We tiptoed into rooms where highly engaged, enthusiastic participants were creating recycled art, practicing ballet, singing, composing music on a keyboard.

"There's much more," Jenny said. "We have acting, fitness, and Hebrew classes. Do you see those rooms? They're very special. That's where former prisoners of the ghettos and concentration camps meet. They can access the archives, and, most joyful of all, they can dance. They have a group called Fire and the oldest dancers are in their 90's. One of them is a Righteous of the Nations, an honorific given by Israel to non-Jews who risked their own lives to save Jews from annihilation by the Nazis."

I immediately thought of Nina and her family. Although they were never officially named among the Righteous of the Nations, they put themselves in great peril by saving several Minkowitz Jews from extermination. I hoped she had felt, while I sat beside her in the shadow of the hill where her Jewish friends and neighbors were massacred, how deeply I respected her.

My reflections were interrupted by two bubbly girls who came waltzing down the hall; they waved to Jenny before they entered a classroom.

"Some of the people who come here have a long heritage, while others have just one Jewish grandparent. Many are connecting for the first time in their lives to their culture, history, and religion. More than a quarter of a million Odessa Jews died in the Holocaust. And what the Nazis didn't do, the Soviets did. Today there are about 35,000 Jews in the city, out of a population of a million. They are rising out of the ashes of their past. Odessa now has two Orthodox synagogues, a Reform synagogue, kosher restaurants, several Jewish Community Centers, and two Jewish universities."

"Take that and let it rattle around in your bones, Herr Hitler!" I thought. "And you, too, Josef Stalin, the butcher!"

Just as I have been digging in my past all my life to enrich and add meaning to the present, I was witnessing a community doing the same thing, on a much larger scale. So much information was lost to them. So many had died, taking with them precious and irretrievable information about customs, food, festivities, the details of daily life. Buildings had been bombed and razed, whole families and communities disappeared from the face of the earth. They were like me; holding onto the few facts they knew, slowly amplifying the stories around them.

"I am so glad we got to see this," I whispered to Paul.

"Me too," he agreed.

"There was no Jewish life left here during the Soviet period, when I was raised. I am the first person in my family to be observant," Jenny revealed. "I tell my mother about Jewish law and customs. I also tell my sister, who is ten years older than I am. She's not interested in anything Jewish. She has a Gentile husband and raises her kids as Gentiles."

Jenny told us that the building we were in was the synagogue of the *shochets,* or ritual slaughterers. There used to be 127 synagogues—for tailors, butchers, for people from different origins and professions. "About 300 people used to pray in this synagogue," Jenny said, "and the person in charge was killed along with his family. The synagogue became a sports club where they learned parachute jumping. In the 1950's, it became a KGB listening center, a communications center for spying on, and bugging people. It was close to a hotel where foreigners stayed, so they could bug their rooms. After 1991, when the Soviet occupation ended, it was given back to the Jews. Not to religious people, but to the community. There's really nothing left of the original synagogue. But we're very proud of the building, which is 102 years old."

A hundred and two?" I exclaimed. "That's when my grandmother left her *shtetl* to go to the United States. One hundred and two years ago."

Jenny's eyes grew wide. She wanted to know everything about my grandmother and Minkowitz. The whole story came pouring out. "This is fascinating, fascinating," Jenny said. It never occurred to me that a young, Ukrainian woman would be interested in my story. "A lot of people everywhere would be interested in your story," Jenny said. "I will tell your six facts to my friends, and they will tell other people. Those six facts will not die. They are part of who we are."

Jenny reached out for my hands at the same moment I reached for hers.

"It's like you two are old friends who found each other after a long time," Alex said. "And you both feel connected to six facts that you learned from your grandmother."

I stared at Alex, surprised. It was such a personal, emotional observation from our scholarly guide.

When we left Jenny, it was so hot outside we couldn't walk the streets any more for fear of melting in a burst of spontaneous combustion. We stopped in at a wax museum, for a little mindless entertainment, but on this trip, our heritage followed us everywhere. Near the entrance to the museum is a figure of a Jewish gangster named Mishka Yaponchik, who lived during my grandmother's lifetime. He patronized artists, and tried hard not to kill other humans. He liberated inmates from Odessa prison and was the prototype for Isaak Babel's character named Benya Krik.

"Good Jews, bad Jews, kind ones and crazy ones, rich and poor, criminals and philanthropists, rogues and rabbis . . . they came in all stripes," I muttered to Alex. "I always thought of Minkowitz as a replica of Anatevka, the *shtetl* in *Fiddler on the Roof.* There were milkmen and housewives, vendors and Torah scholars. They fretted about their families, celebrated the holidays, and kicked up their heels when they danced the *kazatzka*. Before our trip it never would have occurred to me that Old World Jews were crooks and industrialists, prostitutes, murderers, gangsters, radicals, social reformers, artists and artful dodgers, and secular people like me."

Alex nodded. "You understand very well. And now I understand what you mean when you talk about 'emotional genealogy.' You are interested in the feelings, not just the facts."

"Yes," I said. "Yes." I wanted to hug him.

That night was the last time we saw Alex. Vitaly was going to drive us to the airport the next day, and Alex had to stay in the city to finish an archival research project.

"We're going to miss you," I said to our encyclopedic guide.

"You have really knocked yourself out for us," Paul added.

Alex stood very close to me and said he had something to tell me. He looked down, struggling to gather his thoughts and choose his words carefully. "I think this whole trip was guided," he said, "and not just by me. It's like there was divine intervention, and even though I'm not sure I believe in it, I have seen it with my own eyes. Everything happened at the moment you needed it to. People showed up magically. It was like being in a dream. And I have to tell you something very personal. When I ride in a car, I always have pain in my back. But since I met you, I have been without any back pain. I think you are a magician."

My pen pal Andrew was right. Alex had stepped out of his academic, informational comfort zone and his heart opened up. He became much more than a guide. He was a friend.

And, he wasn't the only one who opened up. So did Paul. The last night in Odessa, he put words to his feelings for the first time.

"I thought I was going to Minkowitz and Ukraine for you, to support you, but it turned out to be important for me, too. My grandparents and their lives in the Old Country were an abstraction to me before. Now I realize they were people with a daily life, with joys and pains, triumphs and disappointments. I wonder what it was like for them to sail to a new country where they didn't know the culture or the language. I'm sad about what I missed growing up, and angry that my mother scorned my *shtetl* grandparents on my father's side and selfishly kept me from them. I also have to forgive myself for not finding out more and for not asking questions. I was a little kid, and my mother's disdain for my grandparents made me cautious around them."

"Of course," I whispered.

"I'll probably never know if my ancestors came from or lived in Minkowitz," Paul said. "But it no longer matters. The culture of the *shtetl*s was the same. I came from the same world as you did. We are connected from the past, just like we always thought we were."

Then Paul, who is not a weepy kind of guy, got teary for the third time on the trip. "A part of my heart I didn't know I had opened up. Like Jiffy popcorn, it just keeps expanding. In Minkowitz, with the Russians, I got to toast my grandparents. I acknowledged them. That was very important for me. And we have the spoon from Minkowitz. It was part of our wedding, part of our past, our present, and our future. We have been and are linked forever."

We hugged, two sweaty bodies bonded with the crazy glue of heritage, on a steamy summer night.

After Paul drifted off to sleep, I lay awake, thinking of our marriage, our ancestral connection, and how extraordinary it was that we had found each other. Then I thought of my parents' marriage, and fingered the diamond pendant that hung from a silver chain around my neck. It was given to me as a gift by my mother, when I returned to the United States after living in Europe and North Africa for close to a decade. "It's my wedding ring," she had said. "I had it made into a necklace for you."

I knew how important the ring was to her. And I understood that no matter how hard our relationship has been, we will always be linked by blood, and by a sad, deep love.

Soon after, I fell asleep.

The next day, there was total chaos and no air conditioning at the Odessa airport. Our flight was delayed. We walked outside, through a parking lot to a Georgian restaurant to get take-out food for the plane. It was the last time I would walk on Ukrainian soil.

Suddenly, I felt as though there were people behind me, following me. I turned around, but no one was there. I continued walking. Again, I felt the presence of a lot of people in my wake. I spun around and was greeted by a chorus of voices. Although I didn't see anybody, I heard the Eastern European ancestors of many people like me calling out. "Remember us. Don't forget us. Our story needs to be heard. Write our story. Write your story."

And so I have.

ABOUT THE AUTHOR

Judith Fein lives to leave. An award-winning travel journalist, she is either on the road or on her computer. She has contributed to more than 100 international publications, including the *Los Angeles Times, Boston Globe, Dallas Morning News, National Geographic Traveler, the Jerusalem Post, Hemisphere, Islands, New Mexico Magazine, Travel Age West, Organic Spa,* and *Spirituality and Health.* She is the author of the acclaimed book, *Life is a Trip: The Transformative Magic of Travel.* Judith is a keynote presenter for many conferences, including the Adventure Travel Trade Association, TEDx San Miguel de Allende, Learning Connections, the Texas-New Mexico Hospice Organization, the Foundation for San Luis Obispo County Public Libraries, and many synagogues, cultural, historical, and interfaith events. Widely lauded lauded as a speaker and storyteller, she is a frequent guest on broadcast media, was a regular contributor to *The Savvy Traveler* for six years, and has been heard on the BBC, *All Things Considered,* and *Marketplace.* With her photojournalist husband Paul Ross, she teaches public speaking and creativity as applied to writing, PR and Marketing. Judith is the co-founder and executive editor of the award-garnering experiential travel blog, www.YourLifeisaTrip.com, which has more than 125 contributors. She blogs about travel for *The Huffington Post* and *Psychology Today,* and occasionally she and Paul Ross take open-hearted people on very unusual trips. In her LBTW (Life Before Travel Writing), Fein ran a theatre company in Europe, lived in Africa, and then worked as a Hollywood screenwriter, playwright, and theatre director in the U.S.A. Like a modern-day Marco Polo or Ibn Batuta, Fein has traveled from Mog Mog to Vanuatu, trained as assistant to a Mexican healer, purchased a camel in Tunisia, danced with spirits in Brazil and a Mayan elder in Quintana Roo, dragged her husband to consult with a Zulu *sangoma* in South Africa, swum with beluga whales, had a private audience with the High Priest of the Ancient Israelite Samaritans, appeased the mischievous *jinns* in Morocco, and eaten porcupine, albeit not with relish, in Vietnam. Her website is www.GlobalAdventure.us.

DISCLAIMER BY THE AUTHOR

I have once or twice changed the order of my visits to different towns in Ukraine. I opted for emotional order, because that is where the truth of my story lies.

Esther Kornbluth Kriegsfeld Greenspan, the inspiration for this book

ACKNOWLEDGEMENTS AND THANKS

Nancy King, you have been with me throughout the writing of this book. You are not only my friend, but you became my editor, nudging me always to go deeper, get more personal, and commenting on each chapter with minute and meticulous detail. Your constant prodding gave me insight and courage. You are a remarkable reader who stands, always, in her truth.

To my friends, who have supported me in my quest for knowledge of who I am, where I come from, and my stubborn determination to find peace with my mother.

Special thanks to Aysha Griffin, Debbie Band, Kate Buckley, Jade Gordon, Ellen Valade, Andrew Adleman, Barbara Walzer, Kitt Miller, Phyllis Wolf, Donna Rosenthal, and Harriet Levine for their support, ideas, and encouragement. And to Marlan Warren for her wonderful marketing skills, Margie Baxley for making the book publication ready, and Laura Beausire for proofreading.

To Bob Linden and Diego Mulligan, who died while I was writing this book, whose absence is very painful, and who have now become the ancestors.

To Andrew, my pen pal, and his wife Oksana.

To all the people mentioned in the book who gave generously of their time, information and stories.

To all our ancestors in the former Pale of Settlement.

To all our ancestors, everywhere.

And to Esther Kornbluth Kriegsfeld Greenspan, my grandmother, who gave birth to my mother, who gave birth to me, and, years after her death, continues to inspire me.

Praise for *The Spoon from Minkowitz*

"Judith Fein has created a deeply moving and highly informative testament to the power of memory and love."

—RICHARD ZIMLER, author of *The Warsaw Anagrams* and *The Last Kabbalist of Lisbon*

"The Spoon from Minkowitz is a spiritual excavation, mining a sense of self and place in history through Fein's search for her Jewish roots. Her book speaks to our universal need to belong, and Fein's voice is exquisite."

–SUZETTE MARTINEZ STANDRING, syndicated columnist and blogger, Patriot Ledger, GateHouse Media

"Judith Fein is a travel writer of the soul. As she reveals hers, she takes us on a journey that calls forth our own inner travels. In her intimate voice that challenges us to explore the hidden landscapes within, we hear how one's story encourages all stories. Fasten your seatbelt and get ready to discover unexplored territory for her and for you."

—RABBI MALKA DRUCKER, author of PEN award-winner *White Fire: A Portrait of Women Spiritual Leaders in America*

"Judith Fein is an extraordinarily gifted storyteller who evokes sweet laughter and bittersweet tears, sympathy and empathy, unending curiosity, and deepest love. Her search for her ancestral home becomes a spiritual journey filled with deep poignancy, great joy, and profound learning. We are the happy companions who travel with her, join her in her quest, and exult in her discoveries, as Judith teaches each of us how to become both a devoted descendant, and, eventually, a worthy ancestor.

—RABBI WAYNE DOSICK, Ph.D, author of *Living Judaism* and *The Real Name of God*

"Although nothing is better than a first- hand trip to find documentation of your ancestors' lives, Judith Fein's description of her journey is a very close second. Judith's writing is so descriptive that I could almost hear the conversations she relates in her narrative. The emotions she reveals, her painstaking work digging ever deeper to get to the bottom of the few stories she knew, reminds me of my own adventures seeking my ancestral roots, and makes me want to get on a plane and again head for Eastern Europe to find out more! A must-read for anyone interested in finding their roots."

—DR. JANETTE SILVERMAN, JewishGen Ukraine Coordinator

"Judith Fein pulls the reader into her passionate journey for her maternal roots by telling her story (which she calls "emotional genealogy"). She shares her childhood fears, abuse and anger that became adult insecurities and traumas, and places them in the context of her excursion to the Ukraine to walk in the steps of her ancestors. Her journey has a divine guidance because the right people always seem to appear at the right time. She works tidbits of her life and the lives of her family into the larger history of the Jews in the Ukraine— not just the pain and devastation, but also the hope and joy in rebuilding and reconnecting in the now. By the end, she realizes it is not just about Minkowitz; it is about the total experience of the people from whom she came."

—BENNETT GREENSPAN, President, Family Tree DNA (familytreedna.com)

"In this deliciously written memoir, Judith Fein manages to evoke hilarity and pathos, provide juicy bits of history and cultural insights, and remind us that no matter how rootless we may feel we all come from somewhere, and our ancestors matter. *We* matter. Judith's journey connected to my own rich and hidden Eastern European Jewish ancestry for the first time. What a gift!"

—MIRABAI STARR, author of *God of Love: A Guide to the Heart of Judaism, Christianity & Islam*

"Humans aren't trees; yet we do have roots. Our roots are made of story, memories recalled or concocted, and place both real and virtual. Our roots are imaginal and yet no less life giving than those of a tree. Judith Fein's The Spoon from Minkowitz is a powerful reminder of roots, and a compelling invitation to find your way to them."

—RABBI RAMI SHAPIRO, author of *Perennial Wisdom for the Spiritually Independent*

"*The Spoon from Minkowitz* held my rapt attention from start to finish. Like a harmonic piece of music, it flowed delightfully from major to minor moods and authentic emotions, sprinkled with solid information from a seasoned travel writer. Each chapter surged with both pathos and humor and drew me deeper and deeper into the search for Minkowitz, both in its geographical ambience and its inner depths of meaning. It reminds me of *Everything is Illuminated* in its multi layers of both resistance and fascination with one individual's historical and psycho-spiritual roots. It left me with a greater sensitivity to family dynamics and at the same time a sense of wonder about the mystery of it all. Definitely a satisfying, worthwhile, and even transformative read.

—YEHUDIS FISHMAN, scholar and teacher of Torah and Hassidic writings

"Each chapter brings to life a piece of my past, and with it a sense of spiritual healing and fulfillment. While healing the body is what I have done throughout my life as a physician, I have now been able to heal my own heart and soul, as I have finally been able to bridge the chasm that existed between my present life and my familial roots. Her journey is a must-read for anyone whose roots arise from Eastern Europe, for she brings your heritage right to your doorstep. Hers is simply an amazing true story of courage and persistence."

—CHARLES POSTERNACK, MD, FACP, FRCPC
Chief Medical Officer, Boca Raton Regional Hospital
Associate Dean of Academic Affairs, Charles E. Schmidt College of Medicine, Florida Atlantic University

"The author's passion for uncovering the past will appeal to a diverse array of ethnicities. I see my own family reflected in the mirror of Minkowitz. Shaped by wars, pogroms, expulsions, loss, poverty, and immigration, Judith Fein is the keeper of the wisdom, humor, mysticism, superstitions and synchronicities of her ancestors. I still taste and smell the chicken soup. The author took me on a journey to find herself and I emerged with a deeper appreciation of who I am and where I come from."

—ANDREA CAMPBELL, PhD, psychologist who consults with ancestors in her practice

"From six clues provided by her grandmother, Judith Fein discovers her deep Jewish roots in a Ukrainian village. More than that, she finds her spiritual center and lets readers share her heart's journey. This is a compelling book that moves well beyond the borders of Judaism and even beyond Holocaust history to a universal story of love."

—BILL TAMMEUS, former *Kansas City Star* Faith section columnist, former President of the National Society of Newspaper Columnists and co-author of *They Were Just People: Stories of Rescue in Poland During the Holocaust*

DISCUSSION GUIDE

1. Why do you think the author was so interested in Minkowitz when she was a child?

2. Was there something that intrigued you when you were young? If so, were you encouraged or discouraged about pursuing your interest?

3. Do you have a sense that you have a mission or destiny in life?

4. People seem to show up when the author needs them. How do you explain this?

5. Is there a particular ancestor to whom you feel drawn? Do you know why?

6. Do you think we owe anything to our ancestors?

7. What is your legacy as a future ancestor?

8. What are the different kinds of love explored in the book?

9. What behaviors or traits have been passed down in your family and how did they impact you?

10. Why do you think the author didn't give up her quest?

11. Have you ever been on a quest? Did you find what you were looking for?

12. Did you have the kinds of parents you needed?

13. If you could say one thing to your ancestors, what would it be?

14. Would you want to visit the place your ancestors came from?

15. Do you think it is possible to communicate with those who are deceased?

Made in the USA
Charleston, SC
24 October 2015